NATURE IN ART

NATURE IN ART

A Celebration of 300 Years of Wildlife Paintings

David Trapnell

DAVID & CHARLES

Newton Abbot · London

Frontispiece: *Home Field – Canada Geese*
ELIZABETH GRAY (1928–)
Watercolour, 48.3×72.8 cm (19×28¾ in)

British Library Cataloguing in Publication Data

Trapnell, Dr David
    Nature in art: The collection of The Society for
    Wildlife Art of the Nations.
    I. Title
    758

    ISBN 0-7153-9333-2

Book designed by Michael Head

Typeset by Ace Filmsetting Ltd, Frome
and printed in Singapore by CS Graphics Pte Ltd
for David & Charles plc, Brunel House, Newton Abbot, Devon

CONTENTS

FOREWORD

by HRH Princess Alexandra

As President of World Wide Fund for Nature UK, I welcome this important new art book. It helpfully draws attention to this Planet's creatures and I hope it will also encourage people to appreciate their natural heritage.

Alexandra

PREFACE

by Lady Scott

It is my pleasure, as President of the Society for Wildlife Art of the Nations, usually known by its acronym 'SWAN', to write this foreword. My late husband, Sir Peter Scott, was President from its beginning in 1982 until his death in 1989. He had been happy to support the idea of a wildlife art collection from the earliest days when David Trapnell came to him to expound his concept. But without David's patience, initiative, hard work and tireless enthusiasm the project would never have got off the ground.

SWAN was founded to create and manage a museum, the first of its kind anywhere, dedicated to the study and exhibition of an international collection of fine wildlife art in all media from all periods. In June 1988 Peter and I attended the opening, by HRH Princess Alexandra, of The International Centre for Wildlife Art, NATURE IN ART, which SWAN had established at Wallsworth Hall in Gloucestershire. After the opening Peter wrote to David, ending his letter 'I was proud to be part of SWAN.' I too feel proud to be part of it and hope this book will serve to attract people to visit the museum and see the ever-growing collection of treasures there.

Since the idea for such a museum was new, it is not surprising that there has so far been no general, introductory book on the subject, even though there have been many texts on specialised aspects of it. So I welcome this book, which celebrates an important and exciting new concept and the recognition of a genre of art that has been unrecognised for too long.

Philippa Scott

CELEBRATION

Paintings with messages of cynicism and protest are quickly tiresome and do not last. The finest of paintings are always in celebration . . .

Raymond Ching,
STUDIES AND SKETCHES OF A BIRD PAINTER
(1982)

Celebration is an appropriate reaction to the discovery of treasure. Whether some ancient marine artefact has been rescued from the depths of the sea as a result of painstaking research in ancient manuscripts and charts and then of patient exploration of the seabed, or whether some observant walker has accidentally and unexpectedly noticed treasure lying in a ploughed field, joyful satisfaction is indeed appropriate.

The pleasure that comes on these occasions is not for the finders alone. It is subsequently shared by countless others as the significance of the find, its beauty and its relevance gradually become known to the public. First, there are the newspaper reports, then there may be more detailed communications in learned journals and, probably most significantly from the public's point of view, new books, radio and television programmes describe the details and significance of the discovery.

This book is a celebration of the discovery of treasure that has been lying scattered in full public view, some of it for many years. Whatever the reason, the fact that the treasure was there had largely escaped notice. An exhibition here and a publication there might have suggested that such a fascinating and fruitful field of artistic study should exist. But it is only in the last few years that the evidence has accumulated sufficiently to cause the establishment of an international art museum entirely dedicated to this newly recognised genre of art.

In England the term 'gallery' may mean a commercial enterprise selling art, or a complete art museum, or a room within one. To avoid any misunderstanding, the term 'museum' is used here. The International Centre for Wildlife Art, usually, and hereafter in this book, known by its shorter name NATURE IN ART (in capitals to distinguish it from this book), is owned and managed by a charitable society known by its friends, and described here, by its brief acronym SWAN (the Society for Wildlife Art of the Nations). Even though some books have been published on a variety of particular aspects or practitioners of wildlife art, until the museum opened to the public in 1988 the celebratory theme of this book would have been premature and inappropriate.

Now, at last, this book can herald the work of the museum NATURE IN ART and share its name. Much more importantly, the book celebrates the 'discovery' of this 'treasure' for all to enjoy. The worldwide growth of concern for conservation of the natural resources of our planet and the wildlife it contains makes the publication of this celebration all the more timely.

Is there a deficiency in the art museums of the world? Is the art-loving public hungry? Is it suffering from a deficiency disease? Yes, there is a serious international deficiency. While national art collections in many countries have been notable for the great breadth and variety of their subject-matter and the magnificent quality of the works they exhibit, they have largely neglected works of art depicting nature. In some national collections there are small, very specialised collections of wildlife art, by a local artist, for example. Other than NATURE IN ART, at present there does not appear, anywhere in the world, to be even one comprehensive public collection of fine, decorative and applied art depicting any living (or previously living) wild thing in any medium, from any part of the world and any period of history.

The great popularity of wildlife television programmes, the numerous books on nature now being published, and the worldwide growth of 'green' and conservation movements prove that people now view their heritage in nature with a new maturity, appreciation and respect. At the same time, there has been a dramatic growth in the number of people interested in the various art forms depicting nature. The 'famine' in national art collections is so acute and widespread that every effort must be made to supply what is needed as quickly and comprehensively as possible. While this book is first and foremost a celebration, it is also intended to draw attention to the worldwide need.

No doubt there are many contributing factors which have together produced this international deficiency, not least the frequent dismissal of wildlife art as 'mere illustration'. It is true, of course, that much of the early work of natural history painters was to describe new species in illustrated books and manuscripts. But, just because an artist succeeded in his task of documentation, that is not in itself a sufficient reason for excluding his work from collections of fine art. The quality of a work should be the criterion of assessment rather than the subject depicted or the purpose for which it was painted. The rejection of wildlife art as a fine-art genre has also been fuelled, and very understandably, by the worldwide abundance of very inferior material. Fine work is all too rare. But it is never rational or wise to throw out a precious baby just because there is such an abundance of dirty bath-water!

People are looking for a share of public art-museum space for works of art depicting nature. Even though they have hitherto been neglected in important art collections according to the traditions of the past, wildlife paintings should surely now be made available to the growing numbers who appreciate, and want to see, them in public collections. The growth, all round the world, of a sense of public and individual responsibility for conservation of the environment and our heritage in nature has produced a new awareness of the value of fine works of art which depict living wild things. Members of the public in many parts of the world have awoken, as if from the sleep of centuries, to appreciate the beauty and sophistication of design in nature and the new insights which able and observant artists can bring.

The trained eye and hand of a skilful artist can bring to the attention of many other people aspects of nature which they had never previously noticed. But this spreading of the influence of one person's observation and creativity depends upon the availability of the works of such artists for people to enjoy. In particular, if the public is to gain as much discernment in matters relating to wildlife art as, for example, to the nude model, then art museums must make fine art depicting nature as readily available to their visitors. If the insight of one artist is to be compared and contrasted with that of another, then there must be at least one collection (and preferably more) where examples of works by the best nature artists can be seen and studied on one site. Such a centre for the study of art depicting nature should not only have a comprehensive collection of the best relevant art, but should also provide facilities for academic study, including a reference library.

No such centre existed until 1988. Now one does: The International Centre for Wildlife Art, NATURE IN ART, Wallsworth Hall, Sandhurst, Gloucester, UK. The great interest generated by this first-anywhere centre dedicated to wildlife art, from all parts of the world and all periods, shows that those hungry for this genre of art are beginning to be satisfied. Even though NATURE IN ART has been open only a few years, there has already been a very encouraging response to the idea in general, and to the variety and quality of the two- and three-dimensional art shown in the galleries and grounds in particular. Temporary exhibitions of fine, decorative and applied art depicting nature are held three or four times each year, including subjects as diverse as hatpins and photographs, which add to the variety and interest of the permanent collection. Despite the great variety of media exhibited, this book concentrates exclusively on the paintings and prints.

Ahead lies an endless development of the art collection and the use of it as a teaching aid for the people of all ages keen to experience this genre of art. Special encouragement is given to those whose urban background has starved them of appreciation of our living environment and the young people who are to be the artists and custodians of the world's wildlife in years to come.

A new, apparently unique, wildlife art centre now exists linking fine art in the museum with nature in the centre's wildflower garden and in the reserves nearby. A 'foundation' has been laid on which future expansion and new developments can be built. Celebrating this fact, this book describes the paintings in the permanent collection owned by, and lent to, NATURE IN ART and the Inaugural Exhibition organised by SWAN in 1985. This is not intended to be a comprehensive review of wildlife art worldwide. Rather, it is a personal commentary on a part of a particular collection. I hope that enough will be said to whet your appetite and that you will be encouraged to visit The International Centre for Wildlife Art as soon as you can. Even if that is impossible immediately, seeing the pictures shown here in this portable way can, in part, be like a visit to the museum and serve both to satisfy and stimulate a hunger for more fine art of this genre.

Some artists you might expect to find in a book like this are not included simply because, as yet, the museum neither owns nor has been able to borrow an example of their work. Thus, alas, there will be no mention of great painters like George Stubbs (1724–1806), Jacques-Laurent Agasse (1767–1849) or Sir Edwin Landseer (1802–73). This book describes an exciting, new, growing collection to which the work of such artists will be added. Thus, because an artist is not represented in the collection, that should not necessarily be inferred as a comment on his or her ability as a painter. The works at NATURE IN ART were acquired because they were offered to the museum as gifts, were purchased with funds specially given for the purpose, or are (or were) on loan, having been chosen by the Selection Committee as attaining the standard to which the museum aspires.

If the selection of the works seems biased towards British and European artists, it is only because these works became available to the museum. There is no implication whatever of any national bias or any antipathy towards works from other parts of the world. Far from it! We wish that there were more works from overseas. In time generous gifts and bequests will redress the balance.

Man is a painter and always has been. As early as 25,000 BC the subjects of his first paintings were animals. If it was man's capacity for rational and abstract thought that helped someone decide to call him *Homo sapiens* (wise man), he might equally aptly have been called *Homo pictor* (man the painter). Long before language was reduced to writing, people drew pictures on the walls of the caves which were their homes.

From the tomb paintings of Egypt of around 2000 BC until the Middle Ages, man's chief topic for his art was man, often depicted in his relationship to God and sometimes accompanied by domesticated or hunted animals and birds. With a few notable exceptions in China from about the ninth century AD onwards, it was not until the seventeenth century that artists turned again to give a significant proportion of their time and talents to making living, wild creatures the chief subject of their paintings, as distinct from decorative details in pictures primarily of people.

It is surely a remarkable fact that, while nature was the first subject for man's artistic attention, it was largely overlooked for thousands of years and has only in the last four centuries again become an important stimulus to his creative endeavour. Space does not permit a review here of the place of nature in art between prehistoric and recent centuries. That has been done by others, for example *Animals in Art and Thought to the End of the Middle Ages*, edited by Francis Klingender, the opening chapters of *The Art of Natural History, Animal Illustrators and Their Work* by S. Peter Dance, and elsewhere. In Europe, while nature found a place in paintings over many centuries, with some notable exceptions, it was rarely the prime subject until after the Reformation and in the seventeenth century.

The pictures of the last three hundred years will be the subject of this book. It is works of this period which form the greater part of the collections at NATURE IN ART and about which most is known. The theme is 'celebration' because the treasure – and treasure it is! – that has been unnoticed by too many for too long, is now recognised as a genre rapidly becoming widely appreciated and destined to have an assured place in the minds and museums of people everywhere.

WATERCOLOURS

By viewing nature, nature's handmaid art,
Makes mighty things from small beginnings grow.

Dryden (1631–1700)

Of all the media used to depict wildlife – and what medium has not been used? – probably none is simultaneously more technically difficult and visually satisfying than watercolour. While water-based media applied to paper have been used all over the world for centuries, the technique of watercolour painting has long been a particularly British skill.

For the purpose of this chapter, the term watercolour will be applied to all media mixed with water and applied to paper. Thus traditional ('transparent') watercolour paints, acrylic and gouache will all be included. With so-called 'transparent' watercolour paintings, light is reflected to the viewer from the paper surface through the applied pigments. With 'opaque' watercolours ('gouache' or 'body colour' and poster paints) the paper is used only as a base on which to support the paint. All the colours perceived by the viewer are those of the applied paint, concealing that of the paper.

Since the international collection at NATURE IN ART is in England, it seems appropriate that we should begin this review of three hundred years of wildlife art with this versatile medium. Watercolours are often thought to be typically 'English' because they have been used by artists over the last two centuries for a greater diversity of subjects in England than in many other countries. It so happens that NATURE IN ART

1 *Turtle Dove*
PETER PAILLOU (*c*1712–84)
Watercolour and gouache, 54×38 cm (21¼×15 in)

In spite of the age of this painting, its colours are bright and unfaded. All the important anatomical features are well shown, better than in some modern bird books

has more works in watercolour than in any other medium. This is not the result of a deliberate collecting policy, but rather, happens to reflect what was offered to, and was within the reach of, the museum since it began acquiring works.

Because a watercolour is old, one need not necessarily assume that the picture is faded and but a shadow of its former self. Some of the watercolours of the eighteenth century were made for collections kept in books or folios. As a result the paper, and the pigments on it, have not often or for long been exposed to the damaging effects of light. The charming picture *Turtle Dove* (Plate 1) by PETER PAILLOU (*c.* 1712–84) is an example of such an unexposed watercolour. The pigments appear as fresh as the day they were painted. The pinkness of the dove's legs has an almost 'modern' look about it. There is great strength and richness in all the colours. Paillou was an astute observer. The richly patterned browns in the wings, with diamonds of black surrounded by a pink-chestnut colour, create a striking image of what is a modest little bird.

The painting was probably done as an illustration, rather than as a picture destined to be hung on the walls of the home of Paillou's patron. Peter Paillou was primarily an illustrator who lived in Islington in North London. Specialising in birds of prey and gamebirds, he worked for Sir Joseph Banks, who sailed with Captain Cook on his first circumnavigation of the world, and Thomas Pennant, who was both a collector of natural history paintings and an author of natural history books. Paillou is best remembered for his illustrations for Pennant's *British Zoology* (1761–6) for which Plate 1 in this volume was the original for Plate 45. However, just because the picture was made to illustrate characteristic features of the bird, this does not mean that the result was not a work of art. The fact that he made a technically satisfactory illustration, even by today's critical standards, into a pleasing composition shows that he was a master of watercolour.

Paillou's work as a professional wildlife illustrator, and that of other contemporary artists, inspired amateurs to try their hand at painting. Very few depicting wildlife achieved a standard that justifies their work being preserved in a museum. But there were some who succeeded. Among these was the REV. CHRISTOPHER ATKINSON

2 *Grey Heron* (inscribed 'female')
CHRISTOPHER ATKINSON (1754–95)
Watercolour, 28×21.6 cm (11×8½ in)

The colouring of the bird is skilfully done but the head and eye are too big. A suggestion of the habitat is shown

(1754–95) of whom, like Paillou, little is known. Born in Yorkshire, he spent most of his life as an ordained minister in the Church of England in East Anglia. His ecclesiastical duties allowed him time to study and paint the many birds in his surrounding countryside. Working in Cambridge from 1773 to 1785 and then in nearby Essex for the last ten years of his life, he accumulated a collection of fine watercolours of the birds of that part of the country. The collection appears to have stayed intact in his family for nearly two hundred years until 1954, when it was sold on the open market.

Like the watercolours of Peter Paillou, Atkinson's works are uncommon (and at present undervalued) and, fortunately, many are equally well preserved. His *Grey Heron* (Plate 2) was rather

more than 'a bird on a branch' of the early technical illustrator. Behind the tussock of grass on which the heron stands, there is a skilful hint of the flat fenland of East Anglia and the reeds along its drainage dykes. The bird itself is well depicted, having the typical posture of a bird waiting to pounce on an unwary fish in a stream or pond beneath its rapier-pincer beak. Here too, the subtleties of the grey plumage, the plumes on the back of its head and the position of the yellow eye (where so many artists, even professionals, have come unstuck) are all correct. Much patient observation of living herons must lie behind this accurate rendering, even if he also had a dead bird beside him to verify plumage details.

In the same period, the second half of the eighteenth century, British influence was spreading overseas, not only in terms of trade and power, but also in encouraging and teaching local artists to observe and paint the living plants and animals around them. Enthusiastic private individuals with an interest in natural history – particularly those in positions of leadership overseas – documented the fauna and flora of the lands to which they went, in their diaries and journals, by words and pictures. These, usually watercolours, were either their own work or commissioned by them from native artists or, occasionally, from visiting European artists who happened to be available.

Nowhere was this more so than in India. For example, Lady Impey, the wife of the Chief Justice of the Supreme Court in India, employed at least three painters from 1774 to 1782. Some splendid life-sized portraits of birds painted by native artists still survive from her collection. Later, other people followed her admirable example. The Marquis Wellesley, while he was Governor General of Fort William, Calcutta, 1798–1805, made a huge collection of paintings. In total 2,660 folios of paintings which he had commissioned, of animals and birds, fishes, insects and plants from all over India and the adjoining countries, are in the India Office library.

Companies which traded with India and the Far East at the end of the eighteenth and the beginning of the nineteenth centuries also promoted the painting of wildlife from the ports and coastal areas to which they went or with which they made contact via the trading routes to the interior. The watercolour by an anonymous company artist of the Indian green vine snake (Plate 3) is painted without any attempt at a background. There is no indication of the countryside or the vegetation in which the snake lived. Like the paintings which Lady Impey had inspired twenty or thirty years earlier, the purpose of this watercolour is purely illustrative. But such an illustration could have been arranged in an unartistic way so that it looked dull and uninteresting, however accurate the colour might be. This picture has in it that essential element of composition which turns the very ordinary into something special. Furthermore, even though the specimen he copied was probably dead, the artist managed to make the snake look full of vitality.

When, in Chapter 4, we consider the emergence of varying artistic fashions and practical techniques in the design and production of prints, we shall see that there was a move from the 'bird on a branch' type of illustration towards the portrayal of a creature in its natural habitat. What was happening in the realm of prints was but a reflection of what was, at the same time, occurring in the world of watercolours. As illustration gave way to picture-making for its own sake and as artists came to be more knowledgeable about, and more expert in painting, their subject matter, so there was a new attempt made to show how and where an animal or flower lives. In short, depending on the purpose for which a painting was made, the subject was increasingly portrayed in its natural context or habitat.

This change did not come about suddenly. Artists discovered then, as conservationists have in the last part of the twentieth century, the importance of studying the biological context of their subject-matter. As we shall see, the difference between one artist and another in this respect continues today, as, of course, does the purpose for which the picture is painted. But even so, back

3 *Indian Green Lonoga Vine Snake* (inscribed 'Londoga')
INDIAN SCHOOL c1820
Watercolour, 40×27 cm (15¾×10½ in)

Camouflaged by their colour, these long thin snakes hang upside down in the forest undergrowth to catch their food. The unknown artist has succeeded in making what was presumably a dead specimen look life-like

Londoga.

in the early part of the nineteenth century, there was an increasingly serious attempt to portray the background as faithfully (but not necessarily in as much detail) as the flower or bird which formed the chief subject. AUGUSTA INNES WITHERS (1791–1876) demonstrates this trend in her painting of robins (Plate 4).

Augusta Baker was born in Gloucestershire, the daughter of a country parson. She married an accountant, Theodore Gibson Withers, and moved to live in Marylebone, London, in 1830. In the 1830s and 1840s she must have worked extremely hard because her output was prodigious. As Augusta Withers she painted numerous illustrations of flowers and fruit for magazines, including *The Botanist* (1836–42), *The Botanical Magazine* and the *Transactions of the Horticultural Society of London*, and played a key role in illustrating textbooks, such as *Orchidaceae of Mexico* by James Bateman (1837–41).

Queen Adelaide, wife of King William IV, and Prince Albert, husband of Queen Victoria, bought Augusta Withers' paintings and commissioned others. When Queen Adelaide gave her an unusual honour and appointed her Flower Painter in Ordinary to Her Majesty, she was understandably delighted. It seemed that a bright career of ever-increasing success lay ahead. Her watercolours were exhibited at the Royal Academy several times in the years 1826–46 and also at exhibitions of the Royal Society of British Artists and the Society of Female Artists. But for all this success, she could never gain entry to the Society of Artists in Water Colours (later the Royal Watercolour Society) on which she had set her heart, apparently only because she was so unfortunate as to have been born female.

Her initial success was marred by hard times later. Following the death of Queen Adelaide in 1849, the sales of her works decreased at the same time as her husband's health deteriorated. When his blindness made it impossible for him to support her, when more of her patrons had died and

4 *Robins at Their Nest*
AUGUSTA INNES WITHERS (1791–1876)
Watercolour, 32×24 cm (12½×9½ in)

Painted in detail, the cosy, compact scene creates a credible and harmonious composition. This is how the eye sees such a limited field and depth of view

12

some of her pupils had forsaken her, her position became one of real financial embarrassment. In her last letter to Queen Victoria's Privy Purse staff she says, 'I am positively pennyless and nearly starving . . .'

Jane Austen's character, Miss Bingley, expressed an idea that was held firmly from the end of the eighteenth century until well into the twentieth. 'A woman must have a thorough knowledge of music, singing, drawing, dancing, and the modern languages, to deserve the word "accomplished".' Even though so much was expected of women then, they were to keep their accomplishments modestly concealed at home and never to allow them to be demonstrated to the public. Convention in the earlier part of the last century was against women painters as it was similarly against female writers, well shown by the example of the Brontë sisters who were at first forced to submit their brilliant manuscripts under a male pseudonym. We shall be returning to Augusta Withers (page 28) when we look at other flower painters. But for the present, let us pursue the growing interest in depicting not only the flower, bird etc, but also its surroundings.

One of the most outstanding painters of wildlife using watercolour in the second half of the nineteenth century was JOHN GERRARD KEULEMANS (1842–1912). Born in Rotterdam, Holland, he demonstrated a fascination for wildlife and a real skill in drawing at an early age. He began his career as a taxidermist at Leiden Museum, Holland, and then as taxidermist/artist in West Africa. In 1869 he was invited to come to England by Dr Richard Bowdler Sharpe, later to be a director of the Zoological Department of the British Museum, chiefly to illustrate books. His output was as prodigious as his work was skilful. In all he is known to have his illustrations in no fewer than 146 books and 132 learned journals. He had more than 5,400 pictures published as illustrations in books and journals, an astonishing record that few would want to try to beat, even today, particularly because he also made many of the lithographs himself. In addition he is known to have produced other works which were never published. It is to be expected, therefore, that he had very little time in which to paint large, decorative pictures which had, apparently, no directly illustrative function. The NATURE IN ART collection is very fortunate in having two such large watercolours, *The Black-headed Gull Colony* (Plate 5) and *The Gannetry* (Plate 6). Each shows technical skill, mature restraint in the colours used and accuracy in observation. Because he usually painted only one or two specimen birds (eg male and female), these pictures of flocks of birds are particularly unusual.

In their biography of Keulemans, Tony Keulemans (great-grandson of the artist) and Jan Coldewey (1982) show how, apart from a few woodcuts and other minor black-and-white illustrations, his works fall into two categories: illustrations for books and journals; and original paintings, usually watercolours. He painted for the picture market only when specially commissioned to do so. So, for this reason, too, such watercolours are rare.

Most of Keulemans' illustrative work was reproduced by lithography. His normal procedure was to draw a pencil sketch of the subject and make such notes as were necessary. The preparatory drawings were then sent to the author for his comments both on the subject itself and on the depiction of the natural habitat in the background and foreground. After agreeing the details, the definitive drawing was made, usually in pencil and watercolour but sometimes in chalk or pastel. The drawing was then the basis of a lithograph, each of the colours of which he drew on the stones himself. He also personally coloured the proof copies which served as patterns for the colourists to copy for the published prints. With the coming of photomechanical methods of printing colour illustrations, Keulemans was the last to provide hand-coloured lithographs for a major ornithological work (*c.* 1912).

Like Augusta Withers, Keulemans, for all his prolific output, was never financially secure and at times was in real trouble. 'I have had much misfortune over the last two years . . .' he wrote to a friend. The 'misfortune' was shortage of money.

5 *Black-headed Gull Colony*
JOHN GERRARD KEULEMANS (1842–1912)
Watercolour and gouache, 59.5×95.8 cm
(23½ × 37¾ in)

The quiet colours and swarming birds lend a realistic sense to this busy scene. The softness of the feathers in the nearest bird is skilfully portrayed. The bird's head is brown, despite its name

This was largely the result of rich people not giving him the few pounds which they had agreed to pay for his work.

Shortly before his death, in one of his last watercolours, he drew his own gravestone on which were inscribed the words:

Here lies the body
of
J. G. KEULEMANS
whose blood
was sucked dry by
mountebanks

These words did not appear on his actual gravestone, for his widow could not afford one and he was buried in a common grave. How very sad it is that artists, whose works have come to be greatly valued after their death, too often have been forced to live and work in financial and personal insecurity.

Following the death of Keulemans in 1912, Gregory Mathews, author of the last book to have lithographed illustrations by Keulemans coloured by hand, wrote in the journal *British Birds* (Vol. VI): 'From 1870 to 1900, scarcely any ornithological work of importance was completed without "illustrations by Keulemans" and his sureness of design combined with a felicity of expression, made his beautiful figures always a delight . . .'

Chromolithography, a printing process in which each colour was successively printed from separate stones, had a profound effect on the quality and price of books with coloured illustrations. Another watercolourist, ARCHIBALD THORBURN (1860–1935), was to see his huge output of illustrative work produced increasingly by this new technique. Born near Edinburgh, he was the fifth son of Robert Thorburn who was miniaturist to Queen Victoria. Robert saw early promise in

6 *The Gannetry*
JOHN GERRARD KEULEMANS (1842–1912)
Watercolour and gouache, 60.5×81 cm (23¾×32 in), signed and dated 1885

Perched on precarious ledges of the sea cliff, these fish-eating birds build their nests close together but just sufficiently far apart to be out of the pecking range of their neighbours

young Archibald who from an early age was interested in drawing and natural history. By the age of twelve he was producing nice little watercolours and his father encouraged him to do better and better, sometimes even tearing up what the lad had done in an effort to encourage him to produce more careful studies. Looking back in later years, Archibald Thorburn was grateful for his father's discipline, training and high standards, and particularly for his insistence on the importance of a detailed knowledge of the anatomy of his subjects.

After being educated in Dalkeith and Edinburgh, Archibald Thorburn went to study at an art school in St John's Wood in London. From 1880, when he was but twenty years old, until 1900 he regularly exhibited works at the Royal Academy. His promise as a painter and illustrator was soon noticed. His first major assignment was to make 144 coloured illustrations for the four volumes of W. Swaysland's *Familiar Wild Birds* (1883). But the turning point in Thorburn's career came when he attracted the attention of the distinguished ornithologist, Lord Lilford, who was working on his *Coloured Figures of Birds of the British Islands* (1885–98). J. G. Keulemans had been enlisted as the artist for this major undertaking but he was unable to finish the project due to ill health. This was Thorburn's opportunity and he was commissioned to complete the work. His association with such a distinguished and exacting author was later to stand him in good stead.

Thorburn's familiarity with bird and background, with anatomical and ecological details, enabled him to depict both so convincingly that he set a new standard for others to follow (Plates 7, 8). The large watercolour *Wigeon and Teal* (Plate 7) was generously bequeathed to the NATURE IN ART collection by the late Sally, Duchess of Westminster, in memory of her husband, the Fourth Duke. Even if the painting was primarily intended to show details of the plumage of the two duck species, it succeeds as a picture because of the restful view of the distant estuary shore. The painting is so big that it is unlikely to have been created only as an illustration and may have been specially commissioned.

In the preface, dated 1919, to his own book *A Naturalist's Sketchbook* Thorburn describes how careful observation of living creatures was the key to his success as a painter. He wrote:

Looking at things with the eye of the ordinary lover of nature, one can only attempt to represent with brush and pencil the wonderful beauty of the living creatures around us, though perhaps more of the true spirit and sense of movement may sometimes be suggested in sketches than in more elaborate and finished pictures. The chief essential is to acquire the faculty of observing and noting down the many subtle differences in pose and little tricks of habit in different species, and this knowledge can only be obtained by patient watching.

To quote the words of the late J. Wolf, the most original observer of wild animal life I have ever known, 'we see distinctly only what we know thoroughly'.

Joseph Wolf (1820–99, see page 72), whose work was greatly admired by Thorburn, lived only a short distance from him when he moved to London and was a great encouragement to the promising young artist. Thorburn married in 1896 and moved from London, in 1902, to live at Hascombe, near Godalming in Surrey, where he remained until his death. John Southern, in *Thorburn's Landscape . . .* (1981), describes Thorburn as 'a very reserved and shy person, quite unassuming and singularly modest when faced with praise, gentle and charming and invariably helpful and kind'. Like Keulemans, Thorburn was a prolific worker. He personally wrote and illustrated five books, the first being the four-volume *British Birds* (1915–16).

Just as Thorburn was assisted by Wolf, so Thorburn became teacher and encourager to others who followed him. Of these, probably the most brilliant but least well known was OTTO MURRAY-DIXON (1885–1917). Born in Loughborough, Leicestershire, he proved himself, like Thorburn, to be an able and keen naturalist at an early age. He imitated Thorburn's style to such an extent, including even the position in the picture and formation of his slightly curved signature, that some have thought his works were those of Thorburn. He showed such great promise that it was a special tragedy when he was killed in World War I. Such was his skill, had not his life been thus brought to a premature end, he might well have 'out-mastered the master'. His paintings are

7 *Wigeon and Teal*
ARCHIBALD THORBURN (1860–1935)
Watercolour and gouache, 53×73.5 cm (21×29 in),
signed and dated 1902

This successfully combines portraits of the male and
female wigeon (*left*) and teal (*right*) with a distant
view of a beach at low tide. Painted when he was at
his prime, this is typical of his bird portraiture and
his landscapes

(Opposite)
8 *Black Grouse*
ARCHIBALD THORBURN (1860–1935)
Watercolour and gouache heightened with white,
51×68.5 cm (20×27 in), signed and dated 1909

Here two males (blackcock) are displaying in their
elaborate dawn contest (lek) for the right to an
invisible female (greyhen). Note the skilful painting
of the yellow gorse flower in gouache

scarce. None surpasses in quality the two charming watercolours owned by NATURE IN ART, *Grouse* (Plate 9) and *Pheasants* (Plate 10). While his brushwork and general style show an almost slavish copying of Thorburn's style, Murray-Dixon's choice of rich colours appears to be truly his own.

A few years older than Murray-Dixon, FRANK SOUTHGATE (1872–1916) had a style of painting and choice of subject-matter that were completely different from those of Thorburn and Murray-Dixon. Born in Suffolk, he lived most of his short life in East Anglia and, like Murray-Dixon, died while serving in the British Army in France in World War I. His *Dick Denchman's Feast – Hooded Crows and Hare* (Plate 11) is an unusually large watercolour demonstrating his free and vigorous style.

Another great admirer of Thorburn, born in the same year, was GEORGE EDWARD LODGE (1860–1954). One of a large Lincolnshire family, he too was a keen naturalist from early youth. He studied at Lincoln College of Art. Falconry was his favourite sport, an interest reflected in many of his paintings. Although he was very versatile, like Thorburn, in using watercolours and oils, as a proportion of his total output, Lodge probably did more oils than Thorburn. He was still painting works for book illustrations at the age of ninety-two. Living such a long and full life, he was able to influence many and to have his work reproduced as illustrations in more than seventy books and numerous journals. His *tour de force* was making the 389 paintings for all twelve volumes of Bannerman's *The Birds of the British Isles* (1953–63). The only text by Lodge, *Memoirs of an Artist Naturalist* (1946), was written at the age of eighty-five.

In a tribute to Lodge after his death, George Bannerman, in *Ibis* (1954), described him as a 'wonderful example of the best which Britain can

9 *Grouse*
OTTO MURRAY-DIXON (1885–1917)
Watercolour and gouache heightened with white, 35.5×25.5 cm (14×10 in), signed and dated 1914

The distant vista, the charming colours and the bird in the foreground admirably combine to make a picture restful to the eye, a scene to delight those who love the Highlands

produce, a sportsman, a naturalist, and a very fine gentleman. No one could meet him without feeling the kindliness of his nature and his great integrity, and all who came in contact with him learned to love and admire him.'

The watercolour by Lodge in NATURE IN ART, *Looking and Longing* (Plate 12), is not typical of his work. The frame surrounding the picture (but not its mount, for conservation reasons) is the original one, dated 1928. Lodge rarely mixed mammals and birds in one picture, but here he does and at the same time (apparently deliberately) he breaks some of the 'rules' of picture composition. 'Rules' for a painter are really nothing of the kind. They are guides to the accepted practice of the time and, as often as not, as much statements of current fashion as of what is 'correct'. For example, in the first part of the twentieth century it was said that a painter in watercolour should never use Chinese white. Perhaps the 'rule' came into being because a mixture of this kind usually makes a clean colour look muddy, an effect which could be avoided if the same colour had been applied to the paper without the addition of white but, instead, diluted with water. Then the white of the paper would shine cleanly through the pigment. Artists break such 'rules' when it suits them. Experts like Thorburn and Lodge did it deliberately to obtain special effects.

One of the most common of these 'rules' draws attention to the size of one object as seen in relation to another in front of or behind it. Trained artists like Lodge know all about this. But here (Plate 12), in order to focus attention on the tiny duck out there on the lake, he makes them larger than they really should be. At the distance they are in relation to the fox in the foreground, they would not appear as more than minute duck-shaped specks. It would be impossible to recognise them as tufted duck.

Slightly younger than Lodge, ALLEN WILLIAM

10 *Pheasants*
OTTO MURRAY-DIXON (1885–1917)
Watercolour and gouache heightened with white, 35.5×25.5 cm (14×10 in), signed and dated 1914

A masterly example of the use of these media showing two cocks and a hen peeping from a depression in the ground

SEABY (1867–1953) lived nearly all his life in Reading. In 1910 he became Head of the Reading School of Art, where he had been a student and, when the University College became a university in 1926, he was made Professor of Fine Art until his retirement in 1933. Even though he was a contemporary of Lodge and Thorburn, his style was completely different, more 'modern' and adventurous. Inspired by his senior colleague, the previous Head of the Reading School Frank Morley Fletcher, Seaby became interested in Japanese wood-block printing early in his career and adapted the oriental style of this difficult craft to his own work (see page 146).

Seaby's picture *Turtle Doves* (Plate 13) is typical of his skilful, individualistic watercolours. The painting is carefully composed, with the impression of detail but without any attempt to paint every feather and leaf. Indeed the very lack of detail in the wetly painted background enhances the portrayal of the two birds on their perch in the tree. As in many of his paintings, much body colour is used and, in places, is applied thickly so that the style is similar to gouache. Sometimes, as in another painting at NATURE IN ART, he worked on holland (a natural, brown linen material) which was fashionable at the beginning of the twentieth century and which he was encouraged to use by his more illustrious friend Joseph Crawhall in Glasgow. These pictures were 2 of 135 by Seaby used as illustrations in Kirkman's *The British Bird Book* (1911–13).

Throughout the history of art, a great painter has inspired, and often taught, another. Such was the case with PHILIP RICKMAN (1891–1982), who was an admirer of his teacher George Lodge. Like him, Rickman painted until he was ninety. The son of a naval officer, Rickman studied art first in Paris and then in England, under George Lodge and then Thorburn. He wrote and illustrated

11   *Dick Denchman's Feast – Hooded Crows and Hare*
FRANK SOUTHGATE (1872–1916)
Watercolour and gouache, 62×111 cm
(24½×43¼ in)

Nature is kind and economical. Here hooded crows eat the body of a dead hare in the snow. They have not killed it but are grateful for it. Note the daring, free use of colours and the simply painted distance

12 *Looking and Longing*
GEORGE LODGE (1860–1954)
Gouache on toned paper, 29×44 cm (11½×17¼ in)

In this winter scene the fox looks hungrily at the
tufted duck riding the water at a safe distance. Detail
is economically distributed only where it is essential

13 *Turtle Doves*
ALLEN WILLIAM SEABY (1867–1953)
Gouache with some scratching out, 29.5×40.5 cm
(11½×16 in)

An affectionate scene. Compare the method of
painting the birds, with careful scratching out in the
feathers and the very successful free treatment of the
background. To see the development of wildlife
painting over two hundred years, compare this with
Plate 1

several books, his first in 1931 and his last in 1979. His best watercolours were as good as the best of Lodge or Thorburn but, unlike those painters, he was not as able as they were to sustain a consistently high standard of work. His *Dark Waters – Goosander* (Plate 14) is an example of Rickman at his best, both in handling his watercolour and in composition.

Like Lodge, Rickman deliberately reduced the size of the foreground wagtails in order to draw attention to the two goosander effortlessly riding the mountain stream. If the wagtails had been drawn to scale in relation to the duck, their size and bright yellow colour would have dominated the picture and spoiled the whole composition. 'Rules' in art must be the artist's servants and never his masters. He must master them and not allow them to dictate to him – unless he wants them to do so! Successfully to break a 'rule' discreetly and deliberately now and again may be said to be a sign of maturity!

Another trend was emerging at the beginning of the nineteenth century. We have seen how the social conventions of the time made it more difficult for women to succeed as painters. Those who overcame the obstacles did so partly by careful choice of their subject-matter. Female artists who took objects home to be painted discreetly there were more likely to be approved than women who worked outdoors in the public gaze. 'Genteel'

14   *Dark Waters – Goosander*
PHILIP RICKMAN (1891–1982)
Watercolour heightened with gouache, 56×76.5 cm (22×30¼ in)

Composition is the key in one of Rickman's best paintings. The distant vista, the dark shadow and the deep water; the duck sufficiently near to have only minimal reflections and the treatment of the frothy foreground water combine to make a great success

15   *Orchid Catellia mossiae*
AUGUSTA INNES WITHERS (1791–1876)
Watercolour and pencil, heightened with white and gum arabic, on card watermarked 1842, 59.5×47 cm (23½×18½ in), signed and dated 1843

Transparent watercolour is here used with mastery, the perfect combination of botanical accuracy and pictorial composition

16 *August*
STANLEY ROY BADMIN (1906–89)
Watercolour, 31.8×40.6 cm (12½×16 in)

This picture of riverside trees shows several types,
with alder and willow in the foreground, together
with the artist's sketch-book. It is not often that the
final painting shows the preliminary sketches!

17 *September*
STANLEY ROY BADMIN (1906–89)
Watercolour, 31.8×40.6 cm (12×16 in)

Each tree included is typical of its species: cedar of
Lebanon; rowan; yew etc. In the foreground are the
autumn fruits of the trees shown in the middle and
far distance

27

pastimes, such as painting flowers and insects, were deemed more suitable for the gentler sex. It is not surprising, therefore, to find that more women than men were notable as painters of flowers.

Among the most distinguished in the nineteenth century was Mrs Augusta Innes Withers (1791–1876), to whom we have already referred (page 13). For example, her *Orchid Catellia mossiae* (Plate 15) shows great skill, in both its composition (through selection of the actual plant to be painted as much as in its positioning) and the handling of watercolour. Whether she was aware of the work of the celebrated and accomplished Belgian painter Pièrre-Joseph Redouté (1759–1840), who made his fame in royal circles in France, we do not know. Unlike Redouté, who specialised in flowers, she was primarily a painter of pictures rather than an illustrator of books. Although she seems to have been every bit as capable of creating fresh, clean and beautiful watercolours as Redouté, she is not so well known.

STANLEY ROY BADMIN (1906–89), generally known simply as S. R. Badmin, was born in Sydenham, on the southern edge of London, the son of a schoolmaster. He won a scholarship to Camberwell Art College and then a studentship to the Royal College of Art. His first one-man exhibition was held when he was only twenty-six. He was a painter and etcher of landscapes, as good at human figures and buildings as the trees and wildlife in the countryside, and a distinguished member of the Royal Watercolour Society. Badmin will be remembered in future years particularly as one who loved and drew trees more expertly and frequently than any other British artist of the twentieth century. His works became famous all over Great Britain when the Shell oil company commissioned him to paint twelve pictures for a calendar depicting the changing beauty of the British landscape throughout the year. These watercolours were also used as posters, in the famous *Shell Guides* to the countryside and in other ways. Shell UK Oil has generously lent two of these original paintings to NATURE IN ART.

August (Plate 16) and *September* (Plate 17) feature both tree'd landscapes during those months in Badmin's native England and displays of the fruits borne by the trees depicted. *September* is a great success, combining effectively the autumnal berries in the foreground with the distinctive form, colour and mass of the different species of trees in the middle distance, and still managing to achieve a convincing vista to yet more trees in the distance. How restful on the eye is the distant vista and 'way of escape' in Plate 16 (compare Plates 14 and 71). In these pictures by Badmin there is much to grip the attention and considerable, but not excessive, detail. Both compositions are satisfying, presenting information without blinding the viewer with so much that he does not know where to look or focus his attention.

MARGARET MEE (1909–88) was born in England but lived much of her life in Brazil where she earned an outstanding reputation as a botanical painter. When she was seventeen she attended her first art school at Watford near London. But it was not until after World War II, when she was thirty-six, that she took her art training seriously. Having attended evening classes for nearly two years, she gained a place at the Camberwell School of Art in 1947, where her main teacher was Victor Pasmore, who had led a group opposing the trend towards abstraction in art. 'Look at the shapes . . . fit the shapes between the spaces . . .' was his maxim. 'Observation is the faculty most open to training' was another. Margaret's later work in the Amazonian forests was to show how she made these principles fundamental to her success.

In 1952 Margaret Mee went to Brazil to help her sister who was ill there. Her husband Greville, a commercial artist, joined her and they stayed in Brazil for the rest of her life, tragically terminated by a car accident when on a visit to England. In thirty-two years she made fifteen epic journeys into different parts of the Amazonian basin, often in dangerous and unpleasant conditions, recording the indigenous plants and discovering new ones never described before. She fortunately kept diaries of all she saw and experienced. In her later years she had become increasingly concerned by the devastation of the forests which she had witnessed and she was an eloquent advocate of protecting this unique environment.

She usually made sketches in the forest and worked up a final life-sized watercolour painting from these when she got home. Sometimes she took plants home with her which were her models and later were grown and multiplied by her friend Dr Roberto Marx, Brazilian plantsman and landscape artist. Occasionally, she almost completed a painting on location, difficult though that was, and put only the final touches to it in her studio later. The story, in the biography edited by Tony Morrison, of how she finally found the scarce epiphytic cactus that flowers only at night, the Moonflower, makes exciting reading. It is an appropriate finale to her fascinating career as explorer, botanist and flower painter extraordinary.

The strong watercolour shown in Plate 18 shows the flowers of *Gustavia pulchra* in various stages of development, surrounded by the tall rainforest trees with their buttressed roots standing in the water. A humming-bird hovers beside its food source. The main subject is shown in detail and actual size, while the background is skilfully sketched without obtrusive or fussy detail. In contrast, Plate 19 shows a most delicate portrait of a slender flower on its own. Together, these two pictures give a strong indication of the sensitivity and variety of her work. Wilfred Blunt, author of the (still) standard text on the history of botanical illustration, commenting on pictures in her one-person 1968 exhibition at the Tryon Gallery in London, said 'They could stand without shame in the high company of such masters as Georg Dionysius Ehret and Redouté.'

Another intrepid lady watercolourist was JOY ADAMSON (1910–80). Austrian by birth, she went to Kenya with her botanist husband in 1939. Her films *Born Free* and *Living Free*, and later books and television programmes, concerning Elsa, the lioness she had reared and trained, made her internationally famous. Joy established the Elsa Wild Animal Trust, based in London, which owns a collection of watercolour paintings by Joy which are much less well known than her books and films. A selection of these pictures, signed simply 'JOY', formed a temporary exhibition at NATURE IN ART in 1989.

18 *Gustavia pulchra* (The beautiful Gustavia)
MARGARET MEE (1909–88)
Watercolour, 76×51 cm (30×20 in), signed and dated 1977

This flowering tree is widespread beside rivers in Amazonia. The dark rainforest in the background is simply and skilfully indicated

Gustavia pulchra
Amazonas

Margaret Mee

29

Ionopsis utricularioides (Sw.)Lindl.
Rio Gumina-Mirim, Pará

Margaret Mee
August 1984

A series of accidents left Joy unable to use her right hand. Undaunted, at the age of sixty she taught herself to paint left-handed. These vigorous paintings (Plate 20), without particular detail, give a clear impression of the structure and colours of the flowers and, one may think, something of the indomitable spirit that made her struggle at that time in life to paint them left-handed. At the age of seventy she was murdered in Kenya.

In addition to the collection of her paintings in London, there is, fortunately, another preserved in the museum at Nairobi. It would be a great encouragement to the Trust which Joy founded if, through this book, her pictures were to create a greater international determination to conserve the flora and fauna of East Africa while there is yet time. Her plea for the preservation of wildlife in Africa was essentially the same as that of her contemporary, Margaret Mee, for Amazonia. Surely, we must hear what they say and apply their message worldwide.

JEANNE HOLGATE was born in London in 1920. Self-taught, she was official artist to the Royal Horticultural Society, London, from 1954 to 1966. After making successful lecture tours of the USA in 1963 and 1966, she settled in Maryland and lived there for twenty years, before returning to live in her native England. She has won numerous awards and distinctions for her work, including being the first artist to win the gold medal of

19 *Ionopsis ultricularioides*
MARGARET MEE (1909–88)
Watercolour, 76×51 cm (30×20 in), signed and dated 1984.

A masterly study of this delicate member of the orchid family. Botanical accuracy has not prevented pleasing composition

20 *Ipomoea spathulata*
JOY ADAMSON (1910–80)
Watercolour, 34.5×25 cm (13½×10 in), signed and dated 'Isiolo, May 1956'

This climbing plant, whose flowers resemble the European Convolvulus, grows on the slopes of Mount Kenya. Without needless detail, Joy conveys well the strength of the leaves and the fragility of the transient blooms

ISIOLO
MAY 1956
JOY

IPOMOEA SPATHULATA HALL. F.

Jeanne Holgate

the RHS in two successive years. *Cup of Gold* (Plate 21) was painted with her usual drybrush technique while Jeanne was staying with friends in Montego Bay, Jamaica, where a 'norther' storm lasting most of a week kept her indoors. The large climbing plant, bearing numerous flowers, was growing near the house. She wrote:

I was able to get quite a lot done. Even when the weather improved, I decided to go ahead and finish it, the final what I call 'tightening up' was done back home – in all some three weeks' work. I always let the flower, its way of growing, dictate the design of the painting. Apart from a bare line to indicate the balance and position of the blooms, that is all the 'lay out' I use. If possible, I usually like to show the flower in two/three or four stages of development which gives a feeling of movement or life. In many of my paintings I introduce suitable birds, bees, butterflies or animals.

ETIENNE DEMONTE was born in Niteroi, near Rio de Janeiro, in 1931, and his sisters YVONNE and ROSALIA were born in 1930 and 1932 respectively. They now live in Petropolis, Brazil. All three are distinguished painters and each is entirely self-taught except Yvonne who spent one year at art school. They grew up in a town with easy access to the wildlife in the forests and the

21 *Cup of Gold*
JEANNE HOLGATE (1920–)
Watercolour, 50×65 cm (19¾×25¾ in)

The flower appears first as a green bud which, over one or two days, swells and turns yellow (*top left*), then bursts to reveal the 15 cm (6 in) 'cup of gold' with its veins of purple-brown. The painting is done with a 'drybrush' technique with thousands of minute brush strokes

22 *Billbergia amoena var Klabini Being Visited by Hook-bill Hermit Hummingbirds, Ramphodon dohrnii*
ETIENNE DEMONTE (1931–)
Watercolour and gouache, 73×51 cm (28¾×20 in), signed and dated 1989

The flower is an epiphytic bromeliad and the humming-birds are specially adapted to feed on its nectar

Atlantic Ocean nearby. Their father, an accountant, used to take them, when they were children, on weekend expeditions into the surrounding countryside.

As they matured each spontaneously showed a special interest and skill in painting and drawing and each found nature the inspiration for their work. While Etienne specialises in plants and birds, particularly humming-birds, Yvonne has concentrated on mammals and plants and Rosalia on plants, insects and fish. The family painting motto is 'For love of Nature'. And they add:

We call ourselves preservationists . . . Through our works, we try to speak for the natural world, to call the public's attention to its fragility and harmony. We testify to the spirituality of God present in the natural realm. And we share in a reflection of that spirituality as we create.

Roberto Burle Marx, friend of Margaret Mee (see page 28), said of the family trio:

They know how to compose, how to grasp all they see with humility and love. For me their secret is their great curiosity before the unknown, capturing all the elements of the composition not in isolation, but transposing and composing them into a single symphonic poem, a harmonious union in constant search for perfection.

Etienne was awarded a gold medal in 1983 by the Brazilian Post Office for four paintings of toucans which were used as the basis of postage stamps; and he was the illustrator of two recent volumes on the birds of Brazil and one on the humming-birds of Espirito Santo. Of his various exhibitions, the greatest success was his joint show with Yvonne and Rosalia at the Hunt Institute in the Carnegie-Mellon Univeristy, Pittsburgh, in 1985 and the National Museum of Natural History, Smithsonian Institution, Washington, DC, in 1987. Of Plate 22, Etienne writes:

This kind of humming-bird is unhappily extinguished nowadays by the unscrupulous vandalism of enterprisers who derespecting Nature, destroyed half one of the last sites of Atlantic

forest in Espirito Santo State, in Brazil, in order to realise an 'agro-pecuario' project. In this destruction of the forest, two more species were extinguished in 1985. These sedentary species which lived in the forest had no survival conditions elsewhere.

BENJAMIN PERKINS made his mark in the art world with the publication of his first book *Trees* in 1984. The pictures for this, of which *Silver Birch* (Plate 23) is one, were awarded the gold medal of the Royal Horticultural Society. Born in Istanbul in 1932 and educated at Sherborne School, Trinity College, Oxford, and the Royal Agricultural College, Cirencester, he spent twenty years as the manager of an estate in north Essex. During this time, without any formal art training, he started to paint watercolours of botanical subjects. In 1978 he decided to use the experience and material that he had collected over the years to become a full-time painter and writer. Since then he has written and illustrated three books and provided the illustrations for several others. The *Silver Birch* painting was made, he wrote,

. . . to combine a pleasing composition with as much as possible of the kind of detail that stressed the individual features of each species . . . [and] to illustrate in detail all the stages, ie dormant twig, swelling and bursting bud, leaf, flower, fruit and autumn leaf, of all the broadleaved trees commonly found in the wild in Britain – that is to say, excluding species that one would normally meet with only in gardens, arboreta etc, but including the native and introduced species, especially where the latter have become naturalised. The drawings were done over a long period, as I was not then painting full time, and were of course all done directly from fresh specimens. I used a dry-brush technique, starting with the palest washes and gradually building up in layers towards the darkest and most opaque colours. I think the *Birch* is representative of my botanical work, which is probably what I am best at, although I have been doing more landscape . . . paintings in recent years.

After training at the Chelsea School of Art and travel scholarships to Japan, CORAL GUEST, born in

England in 1955, held her first exhibition at the Royal Horticultural Society in 1983. She was awarded RHS gold medals in 1984 and 1986, and in 1985 was commissioned to design the 1986 Chelsea Flower Show plate. Having specialised in flower paintings, such as her *Iris pallida dalmatica* (Plate 24a, b), she wrote in 1989:

I came to paint my watercolours of flowers through an intense interest in the various changing forms and colour that compose the life of a flowering plant. My works always depict the subject-matter life size. This achieves a quality of image that can be well related to the original plant . . . It is the atmosphere (of the background) no less than the scientific truth that my works aim to achieve. I seem to do more cultivated plants than 'wild' ones . . . After some considerable success, I felt it was time to take stock and review my situation. I have taken an extended sabbatical to develop my skills in landscape painting . . . and am now back in circulation again and am, of course, still painting flowers . . . My sketches are very simple but do give an insight into my working methods.

ELIZABETH GRAY (see page 45) is a painter better known for her watercolours of birds in a landscape but she has also done life-size watercolours of flowers. Of her *Rhododendron macabeanum* (Plate 25), she says:

I was walking through the private gardens of an estate, near where I live in Gloucestershire, to see the rhododendrons. More than three hundred and fifty varieties were there, many of them hybrids. One particularly struck me. It was, so the gardener who kindly showed me round told me, the largest-leafed rhododendron species in the world. Growing more than twenty-five feet tall, the striking feature was the huge leaves with brownish 'suede' on their under-side. The top surface of the leaves was a wonderfully varied and almost iridescent, deep blue-green. The flowers, on the other hand, were a relatively inconspicuous creamy-white colour and seemed disproportionately small for this huge shrub. I was so inspired by this remarkable plant that I decided to ask for a piece and took it home to try to capture in a life-size watercolour the extraordinary variety of textures on these magnificent leaves.

Of the nine botanical painters described so far in this chapter, six are women. Two of the men were more interested in trees, although very different aspects of them. For Plate 25, Elizabeth Gray was inspired by the leaves (while in most of her botanical works the flowers were the main concern). For the other five women, it was the flower that particularly fired their enthusiasm and was the chief subject of their painting. Since there is a notable dearth of women among most branches of wildlife art, except among the painters of flowers, it may be of interest to know that of the last fifty-four artists who have won the gold medal of the Royal Horticultural Society, forty-six (85 per cent) were women.

It would appear that the social motive in the nineteenth century for women to paint at home (rather than other subjects outdoors) is no longer the reason why they form the majority among the experts in producing pictures of botanical subjects. But why are women in every other area of wildlife painting still but a very small minority of artists?

We return to the mainstream of wildlife art and, first, to two British artists who were contemporaries. JOHN (JACK) CYRIL HARRISON (1898–1985) was born in Wiltshire but lived in Canada from 1912 to 1915. He was drawing birds at the age of six and learned avian anatomy from taxidermy. After service in World War I, he studied at the Slade School of Art in London. His many visits to Scotland enabled him to absorb the 'atmosphere' of 'the high tops' and to convey in his paintings something of the grandeur and height of the mountains where some of his subjects lived (Plate 26). He also travelled widely in South Africa, Portuguese East Africa and in Iceland. He was probably the first artist to specialise

23 *Silver Birch*
BENJAMIN PERKINS (1932–)
Watercolour, 54.5×47 cm (21½×18½ in)

Carefully planned, this picture was painted in the course of a year to show the various stages and colours of the leaves, buds etc, using a drybrush technique

24 *Iris pallida dalmatica*
CORAL GUEST (1955–)
Watercolour, 89×68.5 cm (35×27 in), signed and
dated 1985

(a) Preliminary sketches and colour notes,
44×35 cm (17¼×14 in) (above left)
(b) Finished painting. A splendid combination of
botanical accuracy and pictorial composition. Note
the freedom of brushwork in (a) compared with (b)

(Opposite)
25 *Rhododendron macabeanum*
ELIZABETH GRAY (1928–)
Watercolour, 58×43 cm (22×17 in), inscribed 'actual
size'

Here is real skill in handling pure watercolour. The
reflections on the leaves are created by using dilute
paint to allow the light of the paper to shine
through.

~ELIZABETH GRAY~

Rhododendron macabeanum
(actual size)

26 *Ptarmigan in the High Tops*
JOHN CYRIL HARRISON (1898–1985)
Watercolour, 51×76 cm (20×30 in)

Typical of Harrison at his best, this shows
transparent watercolour used as it should be. The
dark rocks in the foreground and the mist in the
valley combine to accentuate the white of the birds.
There is no added white here, only unpainted or
barely tinted paper

27 *Over the Corner – Partridges*
JOHN CYRIL HARRISON (1898–1985)
Watercolour, 33×45.6 cm (13×18 in)

Contrast is often the key to composition. Look at the
range of autumn colours in the foreground! There is
no attempt to draw every leaf and yet there is
enough detail to indicate a hawthorn hedge

in depicting birds in flight. Where other artists had previously failed (some lamentably so) to make their birds look alive, let alone flying, he succeeded in the particularly difficult task of convincingly portraying a bird flying directly towards the viewer.

Harrison lived in Norfolk for many years and thus had the opportunity to study the many species that live in, or migrate through, that part of England. He made a particular study of gamebirds (such as partridge and pheasant, grouse and ptarmigan) (Plates 26 and 27). The triangular pattern made by the flying partridges in Plate 27 was one he must have liked, for he used it many times, although not always as successfully as here. Jack Harrison was a prolific painter and active until the last year of his life. Barely a month before he died, he wrote to me to say that he would donate one of the watercolours in his forthcoming exhibition to the collection that was to become NATURE IN ART. His widow very kindly honoured his promise.

CHARLES FREDERICK TUNNICLIFFE (1901–79) was the fourth child of a shoemaker turned farmer and grew up in Cheshire. All his later work as an artist shows him to be a man totally familiar with the animals and machinery of the farm, and the beauty, customs and modesty of the countryside. After art training in Macclesfield, he won a scholarship (£80 per year!) to the Royal College of Art, London, where he was awarded another scholarship for a further year exclusively to study etching. It was at the Royal College of Art that Charles met his future wife, Winifred Wonnacott, who had won a scholarship from Northern Ireland. Having worked for a while as a part-time teacher, Tunnicliffe left London in 1928 and returned to Cheshire first as a commercial artist, concentrating his effort on farm subjects for manufacturers of farm-related products, cattle food etc. It was also in 1928 that Henry William-

son's book *Tarka the Otter* was first published, without illustrations. At Winifred's suggestion, Charles offered to do illustrations for the next edition. Published in 1932, this was a great success and established the reputations of both artist and author.

In 1947 Tunnicliffe moved to live in a bungalow beside a tidal estuary on the south-east coast of the Isle of Anglesey, North Wales, where he lived and worked until his death. He was hard work and versatility personified. Etchings, wood engravings, scraper- (or scratch-) board drawings, watercolour (Plate 28) and oil paintings, delicate pencil drawings, simple tiny ball-point preliminary sketches and large finished paintings – all were part of his prolific output. A regular exhibitor at the Royal Academy, he was elected RA in 1954 and awarded the Order of the British Empire in 1978. In 1974, on the recommendation of his near neighbour and friend in Anglesey, Kyffin Williams, RA, he was honoured at the Royal Academy by an exhibition of his collection of measured drawings of birds. He had meticulously painted these over the years as a reference source. The exhibition also included some of the fifty or more of his sketch-books, each packed with detailed written observations as well as gems of real-life sketches.

Ian Niall, in his biography *Portrait of a Country Artist*, shows how Tunnicliffe kept a record of his completed paintings before they were sold or dispersed, by making miniature copies of them. But, because he also kept many of his completed paintings and preliminary sketches in the same files (classified according to the subject-matter), it is not always clear to which category some of the surviving miniature pictures belong. Plate 29 appears to be one of the latter, the finished painting belonging to Bowes Museum, County Durham.

Next, we consider three living British contemporaries. RODGER MCPHAIL was born in Lancashire in 1953 and still lives in the county. He studied at Liverpool College of Art for three years and has illustrated several books. The present financial climate in the art world has so far forced him to do illustrative work, but he much prefers painting large watercolours (such as Plates 30 and 31). Rodger has travelled widely in America, Europe and, particularly, in Africa and received

29 *Black Cock*
CHARLES FREDERICK TUNNICLIFFE (1901–79)
Watercolour and white over graphite on cream paper, 13.8×6.9 cm (5½×2¾ in), see text

A few deft strokes of the brush have captured this scene. The pencil lines he originally drew are not exactly followed with the paint

many commissions from all three continents. The scarcity of published information about him and the brevity of his description of his work is evidence of his natural modesty. Neither reveals his delightful sense of humour. Of *Roe Deer*, he says: 'I don't keep preliminary sketches – they are too scruffy to be of any interest. The roe deer I saw in an Aberdeenshire wood when I was on honeymoon in 1983.'

28 *Skomer Afternoon – Puffins*
CHARLES FREDERICK TUNNICLIFFE (1901–79)
Watercolour, 56×68.5 cm (22×27 in)

The style, brushwork and colour scheme are all typical of Tunnicliffe. Skomer is a small island off the west coast of Wales, the home of many seabirds. The typical cliff-top, pink flower is sea thrift, *Armeria maritima*

30 *Roe Deer*
RODGER MCPHAIL (1953–)
Watercolour and gouache, 46×64 cm (18×25 in)

It is relatively easy to paint sunny scenes but far
more difficult successfully to depict shade. This is a
great success, with highlights in the shaded areas
picked out in gouache. The fiddle-heads of the
emerging bracken fern proclaim it is springtime

31 *Red Grouse Surprised, Red Deer Alert*
RODGER MCPHAIL (1953–)
Watercolour and gouache, 51×76 cm (20×30 in)

This captures the Scottish Highlands absolutely. The
heather and rough grass growing in the shallow soil
between the ancient rocks, the glaciated valley, the
grouse flying away (note the top bird's wing beat),
the stag and his hinds ready to run – all are skilfully
portrayed

HILARY BURN was born in 1946 and lives on the edge of Exmoor in Somerset. A graduate in zoology, she is a self-taught artist. Having illustrated many natural history books, she now specialises in birds, particularly those which live in the woods and on the moors near her home, such as the scarce *Merlin* (Plate 32), the smallest British raptor. She writes:

Over the last ten years or so I have tended to pay more attention to the background setting for the birds that I paint than previously . . . In the case of the merlin, I had happened to get good views of a cock bird rising from the heather onto a twisted stump and, with the heather just coming into full bloom, I decided to paint him with the moor in the background.

The stump he used, however, was not very picturesque, so I went across the moor until I found this incredible stunted old pine on the side of Dunkery Hill. It was irresistible and almost took over the whole picture. The whole of the background and tree was painted on the moor and the bird added later, this being my usual method of working.

44

32 *August on Exmoor – Merlin*
HILARY BURN (1946–)
Gouache, 40.5×65 cm (16×25¾ in), signed and dated
1985

(a) Preparatory pencil sketch (left)
(b) Finished painting. It is well worth studying the
composition. The position of the tree might have
been even better a little more to the right as the
sketch shows it. There is a marvellous sense of
recession to the distant hills (above)

Of Plate 33, *Green Woodpecker*, Hilary says 'I think I
have the balance of bird and background more
typical of my pictures than the *Merlin*.' Here, too,
the whole of the background was painted on location in the open air and only the bird was completed in her studio. She much prefers creating
paintings like these to the 'chore' of book illustration, but, like Rodger McPhail, cannot at present
afford to confine her painting to what she would
really like to do.

Another woman painter, ELIZABETH GRAY (al-

ready mentioned on page 34), was born in Scar-
borough, Yorkshire, in 1928. By the age of four
years she had already shown unusual ability both in
drawing and in playing the piano. She won a music
scholarship to her school and, after studying at the
Royal Academy of Music in London, began a career
as a recital pianist and broadcaster. However, at
the same time she continued her art as a leisure
activity and, untaught, illustrated one book and
numerous magazine articles, mostly with scraper-
(scratch-) board drawings. On marrying in 1959,

she gave up her professional musical career and, after her two sons had begun school, turned to full-time painting. Her early works were in oils but in 1968 she abandoned them in favour of watercolours because, she says, 'I had admired fine works in the best English tradition of watercolours and they presented me with a technical challenge.' A few years later, having concentrated on landscapes, she began to put flying birds in her paintings. Since then, in addition to works in pencil, pastel etc, she has established an international reputation for her watercolours of birds in a landscape, particularly skyscapes. Many have spoken of the sense of light, space and peace which her works convey, and the fact that her flying birds really look alive. Plates 34 and 35 illustrate some of these features, of which she says:

Both these pictures are entirely from my imagination. Unless I have to paint a particular place, which I very rarely do, I hardly ever make sketches or preliminary working drawings. After thinking about what I want to do (which gradually becomes more clear over several days), I begin the painting straight away before I lose my sense of inspiration. Apart from deciding the position of the horizon and without any pencil drawing, I always start in the top left corner of as large a sheet of paper as I can manage and work from there steadily down to the bottom of the sheet, painting in everything except flying birds. I leave these until the landscape is finished. Finally, I paint in the bird(s), again without any preliminary pencil drawing.

When I am on holiday I make sketches of interesting features I see, even just a pebble or some moss, but most of the time I think my 'sketches' are just mental pictures stored away in what my husband calls my 'computer'. I find it needs 'recharging' from time to time so I go out into the woods and hills or beaches and

marshes in search of new subject matter. I am sure that the key to success is careful observation of what actually happens in nature.

Elizabeth has been fortunate in not having to depend on illustration work for her living and, since 1968, has concentrated on gallery-type pictures. 'If I can get the paper, the bigger the better. Watercolours need not be insignificant little works,' she says. Unusually among artists, she gives all the proceeds of her artwork to a charity ('The Speed to Need Fund') specially set up for medical work in the Third World.

34   *Home Field – Canada Geese*
ELIZABETH GRAY (1928–)
Watercolour, 48.3×72.8 cm (19×28¾ in)

The frozen pool, faintly reflecting the evening sky, and the light and shade on the snow are beautifully handled (without any gouache or white). For the viewer, the coldness of the scene is discretely relieved by the smoke from the cottage chimney – warmth is at hand!

33   *Green Woodpecker*
HILARY BURN (1946–)
Gouache, 68×80 cm (26¾×31½ in)

Look at the composition here too. It is surely ideal. If the bird was looking in any other direction, the picture would be far less harmonious. Light and shade are equally successfully handled and the paint is confidently applied in strong tones

JOHN WILDER was born in Essex, England, in 1946 and still lives on the Essex–Suffolk border. He modestly wants only minimal details about him included. Self-taught, he did not begin painting until his late thirties. What inspired him to start was a painting of a greyhound by Sir Alfred Munnings (1878–1959) which, he felt, although it looked 'right', was anatomically incorrect. So John drew it to find out what Munnings had done and why. Less than three years later Wilder had become a full-time artist. He outlined the steps in creating his paintings and, in particular, *Hare Alert* (Plate 36):

The initial drawing was worked up separately, establishing the main proportions and relationships. The outlines and essential features were then transferred to painting paper (300lb . . . NOT; I like the surface and need a heavy paper because I tend to abuse it).

I use a limited palette of gouache – raw and burnt sienna, yellow ochre, plus zinc white and ivory black. I use largish (no 4–6) signwriters' brushes.

Over a faint drawing six or seven pale washes of the same colour are applied to establish the background colour of the subject. I use 'dirty' colours, almost all washes containing black and most, white . . . gradually working from general shapes and tones towards detail by continual overpainting.

When the subject is complete, I begin the background very loosely and in barely coloured water. I gradually strengthen and define the colours and shapes and, with stronger washes, wash over the subject two or three times to unify tones in the background and subject. Then I redefine the subject and add final detail (often drybrush).

Then I wonder why the painting hasn't turned out as I intended and get depressed . . .

36 *Hare Alert*
JOHN WILDER (1946–)
Watercolour, 48×66 cm (19×26 in)

The detail in the ears and eyes is enhanced by the lack of it elsewhere. A skilful and successful study in restraint. The simple composition is ideal, the viewer's eye having no difficulty in resting where the artist wants

35 *Golden Eagle at Home*
ELIZABETH GRAY (1928–)
Watercolour, 110×148 cm (43¼×58¼ in)

Few watercolourists attempt such a vast sheet of paper. The great sense of height and distance are enhanced by the strength of the tones of the eagle shown, with its golden head correctly level, as it banks away from the viewer

Next we consider a different style practised by other contemporary watercolourists. By contrast with those preceding and following this section, we look at some artists who have used a more meticulous and detailed technique. Artists in this 'group' come from all over the world. Before we proceed, it is important to recognise a significant difference between painting and photography. Both are art forms and both have been in exhibitions at NATURE IN ART. But a photograph shows all that the camera 'sees' whereas an artist can be selective, by omitting things or moving them to make a better composition. Thus, in my view, 'photographic' is rarely an accurate or kind description for a painting. What, I suspect, most people mean by this term is 'very detailed'. However meticulous or detailed a painting may be, 'photographic' may prove to be an inappropriate term.

Too many artists in recent years have fallen into the trap of thinking that detail means authenticity of presentation and proficiency of technique. The eye cannot perceive a mass of detail in different positions simultaneously. Whatever it is looking at, the human eye, when focused on the centre of the field of view, cannot see with equal precision in the periphery. As some artists know well, detail in the margins of a picture is often at best a waste of effort and may sometimes be a positive distraction.

Famous among watercolourists who have used a very detailed technique is RAYMOND HARRIS-CHING (see also page 113). His style has changed since Plate 37 was created and he now paints mostly in oils on board. Of Plate 37, where the whole background is more detailed than in many of his more recent works, he writes:

Around 1979–80, I painted the last of the elaborately constructed watercolours that had

37 *Nesting Hen Pheasant*
RAYMOND HARRIS-CHING (1939–)
Watercolour, 71×53.5 cm (28×21 in)

This is so skilfully planned that, although there is much detail, the eye is not bewildered by it. The strong shadows create a sense of bright sunlight. Few would suspect that the scene did not exist but that the whole picture was planned and the bird painted from a dead specimen occupied my mind for more than a decade. The pheasant nesting is just about the last of them and, in some ways, represents them all. It's probably looser painted than most, but this is entirely consistent with the direction in which I was moving and the oil paintings that followed.

I had seen a nest with a dozen or so eggs, hidden among the brambles, years earlier and with such a commonly found plant, I would have no trouble in finding cuttings to take back to the studio to reconstruct this square yard of under-growth. The whole mass of it floated in the bath for three or four days to keep it fresh. Each cutting was taken to the drawing-board and its texture faithfully copied. The pheasant herself was drawn and painted from a particularly beautiful and delicately coloured study-skin in my studio collection.

Also from New Zealand is JANET MARSHALL. Born in England in 1947, she emigrated with her parents to New Zealand when she was eleven. She was always interested in art and tried her hand at several techniques, but without formal instruction. In 1968, encouraged by her husband, she joined her interest in art with her fascination with bird-watching. She started producing paintings of birds and within two years she was commissioned to paint the book plates for the Fiat Bird Series. In spite of a serious traffic accident in 1971, which postponed her work, she recovered sufficiently to be able to renew the field work, on which her work largely depended, and to finish the three volumes.

New Zealand Pigeon (Plate 38) depicts a bird widespread in New Zealand. Of the painting Janet Marshall writes:

Before I attempt a painting I like to be as aware of my subject as possible. If I cannot watch

38   *New Zealand Pigeon*
JANET MARSHALL (1947–)
Watercolour and gouache, 78×68 cm (30¾×26¾ in)

(a) Preliminary pencil drawing. Inscribed with notes including 'Very full leg trousers. Tail feathers very firm. Head very small for size of body. Subtle changes in colour from crimson, through purple, to grey, green and blue, occasional golden tints'
(b) Finished painting (overleaf)

them in the wild I will use video film which, by showing the subject in motion, allows one to obtain an overall knowledge of how the bird moves, feeds, perches etc. Quick attitude sketches are produced which are worked on in more detail in my studio. At this stage museum skins are used to get the correct measurements, feather shapes etc . . . [in] a series of rough sketches, one of which I will choose for the final painting. I will go out and get as much of the background foliage . . . to enable me to draw it in as much detail as I can.

The final picture is only the barest outline, which is transferred to the painting board by means of tracing-paper. Up to this point I have made five or six progressive drawings, including shaded works and sometimes coloured pencil. These are all kept for reference.

If there is any dense background foliage, this is done now with transparent watercolour, to be followed by some airbrush colouring. The painting is now ready to have the main picture applied and for this I use gouache . . .

Another artist who uses an airbrush technique to produce some of the effects in his paintings is JIM CHANNELL. Born in England in 1958, Jim, who has always lived near Dunstable, studied at Barnfield College of Art, Luton, and developed a style, combining detailed brushwork with the airbrush, which he sees as his own. Of the dangers and tensions of using a detailed technique in general, and in *Snow Leopard* in particular, he writes:

I would start with (hopefully!) an inspired idea for subject and setting. Next comes reference collecting which would certainly include photographs and, where possible, on-site drawings eg zoos etc (museums) purely for the fur, skin texture . . . For the *Snow Leopard* a skin was kindly lent to me by Whipsnade Park zoo.

(Opposite)
39   *Snow Leopard*
JIM CHANNELL (1958–)
Watercolour and gouache, 34.5×41 cm (13½×16 in), signed and dated 1983

The leopard's eye and fur are minutely and accurately painted. Look at the snow adhering to the hind paws! The rock spur looks a little too contrived

Having mentally pictured (the subject) . . . I sketch out the idea . . . I find that size plays a large part in how well the subject will work . . . I could not paint anything large . . . and still achieve a good overall impact without having to stand well back and view in the same way as an oil painting, when such detail would fade into the background. This is also a question of strength of colour as well as size of subject that restricts me from painting large works. I feel this to be a little bit of a drawback with watercolour type of mediums. On the other hand oils would not allow me to paint in such detail that I feel necessary for me to do, because I am not only painting an impression of a subject but also attempting to 'give it some real life'. I would certainly not knock the use of oils and acrylics because they offer an artist a great amount of freedom of choice to make some wonderful statements. Perhaps when I have reached a point where I have made my 'statements', I shall probably make use of other positive mediums like oils.

Most of my skill as a fine artist has come out of the experience of illustrating commercially and I think there is a question of distinction between 'illustration' and 'fine art' which is not easily answered . . . With illustration work you are drawing purely to someone else's dictation and it's for a specific purpose, whether it is to illustrate a story or to describe how a snow leopard stands on a mountain. I feel, I cannot really paint a snow leopard on a mountain with the same conviction and reasoning when it is to be viewed in a book for a different purpose than you have meant it to be (if that makes sense!) . . .

I attempt to only paint an amount of detail into a subject and surroundings that you would see in reality . . . Obviously although it may appear that you are trying to be perfect whilst faithfully reproducing colour, fur etc, you are bound to get critics who point out that certain aspects may not be quite correct (in just the same way as I will stand and criticise most other artists' work) and on occasions, regretfully you have to accept maybe something is not quite right the way that you painted it! I do not really see any easy excuse for this though, because having painted something in such detail, you

are declaring that this is how the animal really looks, but sometimes the 'chicken hatches before the egg is laid' and you obviously learn by experience . . .

Jim Channell, like others who paint in great detail, has candidly struggled with a subject that obviously causes him problems. A painting full of detail in every part, however much an impressive technical achievement, may not be a picture that is a pleasure to look at for long. All too often, a technically satisfactory illustration does not make a good picture.

The essential skill of an artist, even one intending to convey the sense of life-like detail, lies not so much in actually painting every leaf of a tree or every hair of an animal; any good draughtsman could do that. Rather the ability of a true artist is shown both by his composition, choice of colours etc, and by creating the impression of detail with the minimum brush strokes and in knowing where to put the detail that really is essential. As Jim Channell knows, those who claim to paint in exquisite detail must beware. Every error will be painfully visible to those who know the subject. Many an artist has revealed his ignorance of his subject when painted from a photograph rather than real life – or has even copied from another artist's work – by including some spurious 'detail' which shows that he did not really understand what he was really looking at, including even copying the mistake made by the other artist!

It was recently my embarrassing experience to be shown, with pride, a painting of the charming European birds, blue tits, which, it was claimed, was a triumph of detailed painting. Alas, it was obvious to me that in one wing the largest bird had eleven primary feathers and its other wing had seventeen! Since the number of both was wrong, the artist showed that the 'detail' was false and not based on careful observation and, furthermore, that the artist did not really know her subject-matter. 'We see distinctly only what we know thoroughly.'

DON CORDERY, whose parents are watercress farmers, was born in Hampshire in 1942. His country upbringing has given him a deep love of nature. From an early age he has only ever wanted to be an artist. In 1958, when only fifteen, he was accepted by the Winchester School of Art and in

1963 he went to study for the three-year course in Fine Art at the Royal Academy Schools. There he was a prize-winner in the *Young Contemporaries* exhibition in 1965. He left with a Distinction in the Academy Certificate in Fine Art (Painting).

After part-time teaching and winning several awards, he turned to full-time painting in 1980. Having developed as an abstract painter at the Academy, influenced by his love of nature and deep concern for conservation, he then began to develop a realism and accuracy which he has used more and more in his wildlife paintings. In 1987 the British Post Office selected his designs for use on postage stamps. Of Plates 40 and 41 he writes:

It is never easy to say exactly where and how a painting begins . . . A single leaf selected from a pile, seen in isolation, reveals a whole new world. The ephemeral aspects of nature are of constant interest – what I like to term 'nature's litter'. I can never resist collecting such things as discarded egg shells, feathers, snail shells, small bird and animal skulls, acorns, fallen leaves – the list goes on . . .

Sometimes, something seen today can be a catalyst for paintings first thought of many months or even years previously. This was certainly true of my snail painting. I have always found snails fascinating and amusing creatures; just the thought of dragging its 'shelter' around on its back for a lifetime is quite incredible! Also, the variations of patterns on their shells is truly amazing.

In many ways I feel that the light effect in this particular painting is as important as the snail itself . . . It is as though it is a painting about shadows, and the snail provides another interesting shadow . . .

I have always loved looking at Japanese and Chinese painting, mainly, I think, for their unusual use of composition and scale. I could, I guess, give a fairly long list of past masters I admire, but of more recent interest, and in my own field, I admire very much the work of Raymond Ching, and particularly the American artist Andrew Wyeth.

I do not consider myself to be an artist-naturalist, for which a good example would be Charles Tunnicliffe. I would say I am much more of an image maker . . .

41 *Dead Sycamore Leaf*
DON CORDERY (1942–)
Watercolour, 25×34 cm (10×13½ in), signed and
dated 1988

There are not many who can see a picture in one
dead leaf, and there are even fewer who can paint
one as successfully as this. Here, as in Plate 40,
textures and form, lighting and colour are its essence

40 *Garden Snail at 3 Upper Cottages, Compton Abdale*
DON CORDERY (1942–)
Watercolour, 26×18 cm (10¼×7 in), signed and
dated 1988

Here is a study in shadows and textures: stones;
cement; snail shell and body; lichens and an old rusty
nail

Hind Foot _____

Fore Foot _____

Snowshoe (or Varying) Hare/ *Lepus Americanus*
OBSERVATION: Kawartha Hideaway. Harvey Twsp., Ont.
January, 1982

Michael Dumas '82

MICHAEL DUMAS was born in, and still lives in, Ontario, Canada. While he was at high school, he took a correspondence course in art. On graduating, he attended Humber Art College, Toronto, and he was then apprenticed to the historical painter Lewis Parker. He has had exhibitions at various important sites in Canada, including the National Museum of Canada, Ottawa, and the Royal Ontario Museum, Toronto. Of *The Sheltered Wood – Snow-shoe Hare* (Plates 42a, b) he writes:

The observation for this painting took place in December 1981 while my father-in-law and I were collecting evergreen boughs to decorate our front door for the Christmas season. Along the edge of a nearby meadow, we skirted an immense snow-laden spruce. In doing so we inadvertently frightened a snow-shoe hare that went bounding away into the woods. Investigation of the hare's hideaway revealed a sheltered, vertically compressed world that served as the animal's winter home; or at least one of several that it would use in the area. Once located, it was a simple matter to repeatedly observe the same animal for further study.

The greatest percentage of my work is based on first-hand observation, either on a casual daily basis . . . or as the result of a concentrated study of a particular species. I depend to varying degrees, on photographs, life-sketches, collected background samples, and museum study specimens in the development of a painting; tailoring the information to my remembered impression of the event.

My paintings range from complete 'border to border' habitat surrounding a subject, to portrait pieces that focus on the subject with little or no background objects at all. *The Sheltered Wood* is a good example of the former type.

Prior to 1986, I used watercolour and gouache exclusively for full-colour work. Sometimes separately, but more often in combination, such as with *The Sheltered Wood*.

Plate 43b, and its preliminary sketch Plate 43a, show another example of the Dumas style. The painting successfully avoids sentimentality and the perils of excessive detail.

42   *The Sheltered Wood – Snow-shoe Hare*
MICHAEL DUMAS (1950–)
Watercolour and gouache, 21×60 cm (8×24 in)

(a) Preliminary pencil drawing (signed and dated 1982)
(b) Finished painting (above). The charm and skill of this lies in its restrained use of colours and the positioning of the main subject far to the right of centre

EASTERN CHIPMUNK / *Tamias striatus*
OBSERVATION: Kawartha Hideaway,
Harvey Twsp., Ontario
September 12, 1986.

43 *Summer Trail – Eastern Chipmunk*
MICHAEL DUMAS (1950–)
Watercolour and gouache, 22×28.5 cm (8¾×11¼ in)

(a) Preliminary pencil drawing (signed and dated 1986)

(b) Finished painting (opposite). Many artists seem to have an irresistible urge to make such endearing, furry subjects appear sentimental, particularly by enlarging their eyes. Dumas has maturely avoided this. The lighting is a crucial part of the composition

TERENCE LAMBERT was born in 1951 and from an early age was often making pencil drawings. When he was aged nine he won a competition for his drawings of birds, but he did not begin actual painting until he was nineteen. He has had three books published and has had his work reproduced as illustrations in many journals since 1970. Having travelled in Oman and Nepal, he has established a link with private collectors from the Middle and Far East. Of his *Night Herons* (Plates 44a, b) he writes:

The painting is a simple one, painted for no other reason than a desire to create a beautiful image . . . Most of the preliminary work was carried out for another painting of a single bird . . . The drawing of this was adapted for the painting of the pair.

A joy to paint with their contrasting blue-blacks, greys, white head-plume and startlingly red eye, night herons at rest are the most co-operative of subjects to study. Research for this painting was carried out at Chester zoo.

The painting is a simple one involving the three elements unashamedly contrived. Herons, mossy tree stump and yellow flag – elements all having a different texture. Although contrived, I feel the 'arrangement' to be believable as a chunk of the natural world. I have given the plants plenty of depth to avoid the common fault of painting the foreground as if it were a screen. It is important that the environment of the painting exists beyond the edge of the work. A large yellow flag (*Iris pseudacorus*) bed choking my garden pond gave me the opportunity to explore all stages of the flower's cycle.

MICHAEL WARREN was born in 1938 and studied at Wolverhampton School of Art, specialising in illustration, but for the next nine years he worked

44 *Night Herons*
TERENCE LAMBERT (1951–)
Watercolour, 71×54.5 cm (28×21½ in), signed and dated 1986

(a) Preliminary drawing, pencil and white crayon on grey paper
(b) Finished painting (opposite). Even though, as he admits (see text), Lambert has contrived a rather unlikely situation, it is successful as a picture. This is a study of textures and forms

as an interior designer in the studio of a leading paint manufacturer. He began full-time painting in 1972 and, having had one-man exhibitions on both sides of the Atlantic, he published his first book, *Shorelines*, in 1984. He uses acrylics and his work, particularly the earlier paintings, shows strong links with his designer background. Of *Goosanders* (Plate 45b) he writes:

> The painting of the goosanders . . . depicts a group of birds on the River Trent. Normally they inhabit the adjacent gravel-pit waters. Due to the cold winter, the gravel-pits were completely frozen and it is then that the river becomes a lifeline for so many of our local aquatic birds . . .
>
> As with the great majority of my paintings, the origination is based on observation in the field. Small pencil sketches are made and these are transferred to sketch-books with crayons when I return home. If the idea is to be progressed I then design a picture with the sketches for the bird used in conjunction with notes, and often transparencies of background detail I need to use.
>
> The painting was a typical example of [my] birds in a landscape. The observation of the goosanders linked to a strong background design.

Michael uses coloured crayons for his preliminary drawings (Plates 45a, 46a), and Plate 46b is another typical example of his individual style.

DAVID MORRISON REID-HENRY (1919–77) was born in Colombo, Ceylon (now Sri Lanka), where his entomologist father was also author and illustrator of many natural history books. After serving in the army in World War II, he settled in Rhodesia (now Zimbabwe). He illustrated, or contributed to, many books, notably *The Eagles, Hawks and Falcons of the World* (1968). He also kept a collection of living wild birds (pheasants, owls, raptors, doves etc); many of them came from the tropics, notably his 'Tiara', an African crowned hawk eagle from which, because no one else could handle the huge bird, he was rarely separated for some nine years. It was his total familiarity with such species that enabled him to depict so convincingly birds like the *Purple Guan* (Plate 47), one of the privileged occupants of his aviary.

45 *Goosanders*
MICHAEL WARREN (1938–)
Acrylic, 22.5 × 28.2 cm, (9 × 11 in), signed and dated
1982

(a) Preliminary coloured crayon sketches (signed and
dated Jan 1982)
(b) Finished work (above). The painting faithfully
records the fact that in snow scenes few colours can
be discerned, particularly when viewed against the
sun. The brown heads and grey backs of the females
and the green-black heads of the males are, apart
from the setting sun, the only colours perceptible

Michael Warren

*Goosander – Cotton. Nottinghamshire.
Jan 82.*

(Opposite)
46 *Kittiwakes. Highland Region. June*
MICHAEL WARREN (1938–)
Acrylic, 40.5 × 18 cm (16 × 7 in), signed and dated 1983

(a) Preliminary coloured crayon sketches (signed and
dated June 1983)
(b) Finished painting. Warren successfully shows a
bird and its chick close-up as well as the height of
the cliff nesting-ledges above the sea

Michael Warren

Kittiwakes

Scotland. June 83.

D.M.HENRY

64

47 *Purple Guan*
DAVID MORRISON REID-HENRY (1919–77) (see page 61)
Gouache, 34×26 cm (13½×10¼ in)

Photography could not fully capture the skilfully
painted, purple sheen in the shot green-purple back
of this magnificent bird. A three-dimensional
impression has been created, with an equally
convincing choice of colours

Now we turn to artists using a more 'free'
watercolour style. PETER PARTINGTON was born in
1941 and studied at Bournemouth and Hornsea
Colleges of Art. He became an art master at a
school in Kent but after some years gave up his
salaried post in order to work full time at his art.
Since 1980 he has exhibited widely in Britain and
West Germany and illustrated several books. In
addition to his visual art, Peter Partington has
written a lot of poetry and specially composed the
following to accompany Plates 48a and b:

48 *Moorhen Nesting*
PETER PARTINGTON (1941–)
Watercolour, 27×37 cm (10½×14½ in)

(a) Preliminary pencil sketch
(b) Finished painting (overleaf). The placid bird sits
on her nest while the rain bejewels her back and
makes rings in the water. Partington is content to
use only the quiet colours of nature

Sitting Moorhen
Minsmere – Spring 1984

She dozes, plump,
Jammed into a socket of grass,
Braceleted with dry reeds.
The cold tussocks around her,
Speared with spring'flags
Pushing against the night.
The evening ruffles her web
And scatters a few gems of rain
Over her back.
She tucks her black head
Under brown scapulars
Into a darkness, where
Her warm clutch lies, bright.

And he adds:

A few incomplete-sounding lines which provide another dimension of feeling recollected, like Wordsworth, in tranquillity. Could the painting itself hopefully generate similar feelings in the viewer?

I am reminded of that wonderful statement by Lars Jonsson, 'a bird in a certain setting, in a certain light, speaks to me and touches something within me' (Leigh Yawkey Woodson Art Museum Catalogue, 1984). I've never heard a better description of the way the artist is triggered into inspiration, and how the artist is a medium for putting into words or paint that which is 'speaking' to him.

I can see the moorhen in my mind's eye even now some years later. This memory is helped no doubt by having painted the image directly I arrived home from the trip.

The bird was a few yards from the hide, sitting calmly amongst the activity around her. Spring-intoxicated birds like Godwits were displaying, Bitterns booming, Mallard chasing. Inside the hide there was an equal human hubbub as watchers arrived and departed.

I somehow split off mentally and began to memorise the birds. I was struck by the warmth of the brown back feathers which contrasted against her slaty grey head; the slash of red and yellow on the beak; the abstract zigzags of reeds which formed the rim of the nest; all, against the dark backdrop of tussocks, irises and dim light . . .

Something spoke – I was thrilled by the whole scene – and determined to paint it. In my sketch-book I made sure I caught the plump circular outline of the bird. Already my fingers were itching to pick up my paint brush and say 'this is how it was'. I put everything into the painting but with dumb grief could not do what I thought was justice to the subject. A second attempt was out of the question, would not capture the immediacy . . .

In 1952, LARS JONSSON was born in Sweden of parents who encouraged him from an early age to be interested in watching, identifying and drawing birds. While he was not an infant prodigy, he certainly made remarkable progress, for at the age of fifteen he had his first exhibition at the Riks (state) Museum in Stockholm. One of the staff there recognised his skill in illustrating birds and it was not long before he was commissioned to illustrate five field guides of the birds of Europe. So successful has this been that, together with the reproduction of his works as prints in North America and sell-out exhibitions of his paintings in London and elsewhere, he has been able to be less dependent on the income from book illustration and to concentrate more on painting large pictures. He has written the Swedish text for, and illustrated, his most recent book, *A Day in May* (1990). He is versatile in his use of watercolour, acrylic and oil paints (Plates 49, 62). He lives on an island in the Baltic Sea. He comments (verbatim):

In later years I have had many opportunities to reflect upon the question: what do I aim with my paintings? There are many things I would like to express but mostly words fall short, and I guess that's the way I paint. To put it simple I paint birds because I like to do so, and because I have done so since I was four years old. When it comes to emotions and deeper layers of my personality and how this might be reflected in what I paint words tend to fail, they always appear fragmentary.

Painting birds, as well as animals or other subjects, fulfils not only one but many needs within me. Painting is a language with which I want to express different sides of life . . . Inspiration can strike me like lightning while watching something but also slowly build up during

på vinterjorden 13/2 -87

observations of a bird species over a long period. Usually there is something, a colourshade, a pose, a special lighting that hits me, that touches something within me.

Very often I paint direct from nature. Painting out in the field includes a certain amount of unconsciousness where it appears as if only the eye and the hand create. It mostly results in a certain amount of simplification or abstraction. At its best it feels as if the picture develops its own terms. The result varies accordingly, but very often a spontaneous sketch communicates back to me, formulating something that I was not aware of. In this lies an important possibility to develop.

Having found something inspiring in a field sketch I often try to develop or transfer it to a larger painting . . . The final results, however, the overall atmosphere or spirit of the painting, develops during a conversation between myself and the work. I find myself aiming at a point where the painting reflects something within me . . .

A penetration to a point of almost identification with the subject is mostly necessary for me in order to infuse a spirit in the painting. This also gives me a confidence or a sense of freedom, as if I was creating a scene rather than copying it. If you try to render the delicate feather pattern of a woodcock by slavishly copying it, it will often appear lifeless. But trying to understand and almost identify with its rhythm, structure and feel the dynamism between the colourshades you can create a pattern that represents your impression of its beauty. You end up painting life rather than making a representation of nature.

49 *Winter Sparrowhawk*
LARS JONSSON (1952–)
Watercolour, 42×56 cm (16½×22in), signed and dated 13 Feb 1987

There is no need in this splendid, freely painted, picture for great detail anywhere except where it has been put: in the eye of the hawk and, to a lesser extent, in the feathers. The admirably simple treatment of the branches of the tree has an almost oriental character

50 *Honey Buzzard*
VADIM GORBATOV (1940–)
Indian ink and watercolour, 26×18 cm (10¼×7 in)

The charm of a picture like this lies in its simplicity of design and colouring. It could hardly be more restrained. Much patient observation has gone into the making of this, both of the bird and the wild wasps' nest which it is raiding

VADIM GORBATOV was born in Russia in 1940. After graduating from art school and studying later at a Design Institute, he received the degree of Master of Art Criticism. Since then he has worked as designer, art teacher and television set-designer and is now a full-time artist. He has illustrated books on nature and travelled extensively in his country 'in search of places where undisturbed environments can be found, watching and drawing wild animals'.

The pictures *Honey Buzzard* (Plate 50) and *Serpent Eagle* (Plate 51) were made as illustrations for a 'popular science' book on birds of prey: 'So my main object was not only to give a true to life description of the birds . . . but to get a reader interested, to make him realise the perfect beauty of these flying creatures as well.'

After making a number of small pencil sketches and deciding on the best arrangement of the subject-matter, larger, more detailed, sketches are prepared and finally a full-sized drawing in pencil.

The extent of thoroughness with which preparatory drawings are made depends mainly on which technique I am going to use at the final stage. Oil or gouache require a more sketchy drawing while watercolours and Indian ink are to be prepared thoroughly since they are very difficult to correct . . .

I watched honey buzzards in various situations – sitting in a tree, while he was flying or digging out the wasps . . . What really impelled me to paint were the wasps whom I met every now and then in sheds or under roofs of country houses. Their threatening buzz so much contrasting with the calm and business-like manners of the birds ravaging their nest is to my mind the emotional score of the work . . .

Generally speaking I think it very important to be conscious of the interconnection between animals and their environment. To display the natural beauty of the animal is possible only through realisation of the world's harmony. The sensation, as well as the painter's ability to retain, childlike admiration of the world of nature, let alone the professional qualities, are to my mind the most necessary traits of a wildlife painter.

As the paintings shown in this chapter well illustrate, watercolours may be used for a vast

variety of subjects and in almost as many ways. They are, probably, technically a more difficult medium to handle than any other, particularly when using the 'transparent' technique. For all that, when they are in the hand of an expert, watercolours produce paintings which have a charming freshness and 'clean' look that is as captivating as it is unrivalled.

51 *Serpent Eagle*
VADIM GORBATOV (1940–)
Indian ink and watercolour, 26×18 cm (10¼×7 in)

Plates 50 and 51 were prepared primarily as book illustrations. A fight to the death has here been dramatically portrayed. The coniferous forest habitat is shown

OILS AND PASTELS

Art should be nothing but the beautiful.

Jean Auguste Dominique Ingres (1780–1867)

As watercolours are paintings made with water-based pigments, so oil paintings have oil as the vehicle for the colours. While canvas has remained a popular foundation for oil paintings, there have always been those who painted on timber, leather, metal and other surfaces. In the twentieth century a popular material has been 'hardboard', commonly described simply as 'board' (or 'Masonite' in North America), because it is stable in a wide range of climates, needs no stretching frame and at once offers two different surfaces on which to work: the smooth 'front' and rough 'back'.

To simplify the divisions of this book, paintings on board or canvas in other opaque media, such as acrylics, are included here, even though they are not strictly oil paints. Acrylics are an emulsion of pigment in a quick-drying, synthetic resin medium. To keep the balance between the chapters, the only pastel painter in the book is included here too.

The technique has an honourable pedigree, having been used as early as the first part of the fifteenth century by Jan van Eyck. The coming of the sixteenth century saw the development of canvas as the backing for oil paintings. As the media on which oil paintings were based varied, so too did the styles of painting. Some artists of the seventeenth-century Flemish school, for example, used a white primer and, applying the paint thinly like watercolour, allowed the background to shine

52 *Peregrines*
JOSEPH WOLF (1820–99)
Oil on canvas, 88×62 cm (34¾×24½in), signed and dated 1866

Painted long before colour photography and good binoculars, this shows the mastery and careful observation which was the foundation of Wolf's success. Note the shadow of the wing on the leg, the loose feathers blowing about and the posture of the young bird waiting to be fed

through the surface colours. Others, like Rembrandt (1606–69), used dark backgrounds and applied all the highlights in opaque pigments. Thus the use of oil paint was already well established when painters, such as Melchior de Hondecoeter (1636–95) in Holland, Francis Barlow (1626–1704) and Jakob Bogdani (1660–1724), both in England, at the end of the seventeenth and beginning of the eighteenth centuries began to create paintings primarily depicting wildlife.

In the art galleries of many museums oil paintings are the most numerous. But in NATURE IN ART this is not so. Sadly, the most important reason for this is the high price now being fetched by first-class oil paintings. The earliest oil painting in the permanent collection is *Peregrines* (Plate 52) by JOSEPH WOLF (1820–99). Born near Coblenz in Germany, the son of a farmer, he became a distinguished naturalist, artist and lithographer. From an early age, he had a special interest in birds of prey. The goshawk which raided his parents' poultry and the eagle owl which perched in a tree near his home created early memories that influenced him all his life. He appears to be one of the first painters successfully to earn his living from the painting of wildlife only.

A. H. Palmer, in the preface to his biography of Wolf, describes how, following their first meeting:

Time passed on, and when, after many explorations of his portfolios, I had formed some estimate of Wolf's power, his ideal, and his life-long diligence in searching for knowledge, there arose a strange, strong longing to make these things more widely known – the feeling and poetry, the scholarly, unmercenary learning, and the consuming manipulative skill, all so loyally ministering to truth.

53 *Peregrine Tiercel (male)*
JOSEPH WOLF (1820–99)
Charcoal sketch, signed and dated 1876

The similarity of the posture to the birds shown in Plate 52 may be accidental. The importance of this is the paper on which the sketch was made, indicating Wolf's use of tracing onto the definitive work (see text)

Wolf was a prolific illustrator. Hundreds of plates by him were published in learned journals such as *Ibis* and *The Proceedings of the Zoological Society*. Several hundred more were in books published over the period 1845–95. Even though this must have kept him very busy, he also found time for major gallery paintings. He remained a bachelor, content with a simple life-style. While he was scrupulously fair in his comments on other animal artists, he emphasised that their failures were often due to the fact that they did not spend sufficient time in the field observing their subject-matter. Of one artist, Wolf candidly commented: '— produced a thing with a buzzard's outlines and osprey's markings. He may possibly draw from life such things as herons which stand like a post; but he does not consult living things sufficiently.'

Of the sketch (Plate 53), Palmer says this was 'the first idea of a picture exhibited at the Sports and Arts Exhibition . . . Like many of the artist's sketches, it is done on thin paper (often whity-brown) [sic], and the outline has been scored over in transferring it.' This suggests that, like many an artist today, when Wolf had found a pleasing composition, he traced it from the sketch directly onto the canvas for the finished painting. If this was his frequent practice, it would explain his preference for thin paper.

Study of an international collection of art makes possible the identification of trends and fashions on a world scale. One is clear. In wildlife art there is an international predominance of paintings of birds as the subjects. This is not confined to any period, medium or part of the world. It appears that birds have particularly inspired artists to paint, but not all birds equally. Some species occur in paintings much more frequently than others and no group is more popular than the birds of prey, or raptors. We begin this chapter by continuing to look at artists who have depicted these.

GEORGE EDWARD LODGE (see page 18), like Wolf, was particularly fascinated by raptors. Falconry was his favourite sport and he painted many pictures of his captive hunting birds. His thorough familiarity with these enabled him to depict them in his paintings (Plate 54) with convincing accuracy.

One of Lodge's pupils was DAVID MORRISON REID-HENRY (see also page 61) who, like his teacher, was fascinated by birds of prey (Plate 55). In the book *Highlight the Wild* by his brother and fellow-artist Bruce, David is shown as one who made few field sketches. After long hours of careful observation, often with binoculars, he stored in his memory all the images he needed. He would go home and make a few pencil sketches of what he had seen, recording particular postures etc, and then he was ready to start his painting. He usually worked in opaque paints: gouache (Plate 47), tempera and oil (Plate 55, page 75). He used specimens to enable him to depict accurately the plumage and proportions of his subjects and often took plants to his studio for inclusion in creating an authentic background.

One using a less detailed technique to paint a golden eagle is LENNART SAND, who was born in 1946 in Sweden and still lives there. He is a versatile, self-taught artist in oils but also makes lithographs and drypoint etchings. His first book, *Divine Landscape*, was published in 1989 with text, forty-nine paintings and numerous drawings by him. In 1987 he had a one-man exhibition at the Natural History Museum, Stockholm, when *Golden Eagle* (Plate 56) was included. He has also had his work exhibited in other museums and galleries in Sweden and the United States.

With the help of a friend who translated for him, he writes:

Painting nature is a way of communicating one's feelings to other people . . . All art is a matter of looking at one's surroundings through a veil of temperament. Nature art is, thus, not just pictures – documentary pictures – but pictures that are coloured by the approach used by the artist and conditioned by his temperament. There are many ways of interpreting a subject and this can be seen with the greatest clarity when several artists paint the same subject. The artist's spiritual awareness colours the painting . . .

Painting nature is a way of life. One of the fundamentals is to seek a kind of relationship with nature. Few people I have met have had that property . . .

My time at the easel, as well as out in the countryside, is a part of my life, which I am glad to share and hope will be of interest. But I must admit that a large part of my urge to paint is conditioned by an insatiable desire to create. There is an immense pleasure in achieving success after having struggled up the side of a mountain with my painting equipment and having battled with mosquitoes and a rapidly changing countryside. Despondency falls just as heavily in the face of failure . . .

I am inspired by the scents of the countryside and by the wind which moves in the tree tops, or by the early morning concert of the birds congregating along the forest's edge . . .

In his own English he wrote to me on another occasion (with his permission I quote verbatim):

I often walk in the forrests around my house and my landscapes is often painted outdoors. Its then easier to get the whole experience through Your eye on to canvas. Its easier to feel the 'atmospheric light' witch was one of the first rules the impressionists created. And You must have a special relationship to the landscape, the environment and its animals.

Mostly I make ruff sketches of my birds and mamals. Just to remember sertain caracteristic parts in its form or in its movement. Then I make oilsketches in my studio from my pensilsketches. But mostly I go right to the oilsketching when I have my experience clear in my mind. My oilsketching is done with turpentine and raw umbra, and when I feel satisfied with the formdisplay and the caracters I start to put on more colour.

An extremely successful and versatile painter, ROBERT BATEMAN was born in 1930 in Toronto and educated there. In 1948 he had lessons in painting from Gordon Payne, a respected Toronto artist. He began selling his wildlife paintings of African animals while he was on a two-year teaching assignment in Nigeria (1963–5). He worked for the next twenty years as a teacher of geography and art, gradually turning to teaching art only. In 1975, the year of his first one-man exhibition at the Tryon Gallery, London, he gave up his teaching career and became a full-time painter. He has had two books published about him and his work, *The Art of Robert Bateman* (1981) and *The World of Robert Bateman* (1985). In 1984 he had the rare distinction of being named an

(Left)
54 *Merlins*
GEORGE EDWARD LODGE (1860–1954)
Oil on board, 29.5×38 cm (11½×15 in)

Here is a fine example of an oil by Lodge, restrained in the use of colour and detail. The composition might have been even more successful if the birds had been placed a little more to the right

(Right)
55 *Golden Eagle*
DAVID MORRISON REID-HENRY (1919–77)
Oil on canvas, 70×57 cm (27½×22½ in), signed 'D. M. Henry'

This is one of the best of his paintings and typical of his careful style. The bird is a little too central in position to be ideal and it might have been better if the brown hillside behind it had been less strongly defined

56   *Golden Eagle*
LENNART SAND (1946–)
Oil on canvas, 200×230 cm (79×91 in), signed and
dated 1982

(a, b) Preliminary pencil sketches
(c) Finished painting (opposite). The second bird in
(a) was wisely omitted. The golden head of the eagle,
which gives the bird its name, contrasts against the
muted colours of the distant mountain. Needless
detail is avoided and the resulting large picture is
spectacular

of a falconer who used it for chasing gulls away from the Toronto International Airport.

There were interesting technical problems such as making the lighting on the bird consistent with lighting on the rock as is often the case in my paintings. The landscape effect is more interesting or challenging than the bird or mammal. It was a great pleasure for me to examine the planes and surfaces of the rock, eliminate some and invent others to make an interesting and harmonious whole. The actual particular forms and textures of the real world are my main fascination. This subject afforded me a very good opportunity to explore these.

I usually work directly on the board or canvas in a very rough and crude way and work out my artistic problems as I go along. A master artist once said 'In order to learn how to draw you have to make at least 2000 mistakes, get busy and start making them.' That is my approach to a painting. It evolves and changes as it goes along.

I work in thin layers alternating dark with opaque lights. Periodically during the course of a painting I may give an overall wash of a semitransparent gray which kills the darkest darks and lightest lights and gives me the opportunity to emphasise tone and contrast as I go.

Officer of the Order of Canada. *Evening Light – White Gyrfalcon* (Plate 57) was used for the illustration on the cover of the catalogue for his prestigious one-man exhibition of 110 of his paintings at the National Museum of Natural History in Washington, DC, in 1987.

Bateman writes of his work in general, and Plate 57 in particular:

Sometimes I do a number of preliminary sketches and sometimes I don't. In the case of the *White Gyrfalcon* I found a particularly handsome rock on the coast of Hudson Bay which was the main motivation for doing the painting. The white gyrfalcon was in the collection

GYRFALCON

57 *Evening Light – White Gyrfalcon*
ROBERT BATEMAN (1930–)
Acrylic on board, 92×122 cm (36×47 in), signed and
dated 1981

(a) Pencil compositional drafts (opposite left)
(b) Pencil posture studies (opposite right)
(c) Finished work. The composition and the posture
of the bird finally selected are well chosen and, as
usual with this artist, the colour scheme is restrained

JOHN SEEREY-LESTER was born in 1945 and educated in Lancashire, England. His art training was at Salford Technical College, where he did a four-year diploma course in graphic and intermediate design. He emigrated to the USA, where he now lives in Florida.

A versatile painter, he now concentrates his work on wildlife subjects, usually using oil or acrylics to depict a wide variety of scenes and wildlife. His *Low Tide – Bald Eagles* (Plates 58a, b) shows his mastery of landscape and birds. His attention to detail in those parts of the picture where it is essential and his skill in barely hinting at detail where it is not, is well shown in this and in *Cougar Run* (Plate 78).

Of Plate 58 he says:

Rightfully deserving its national status, the Bald Eagle is nonetheless endangered in forty-three states and threatened in another five. On a visit to Juneau, Alaska, one spring, I was amazed at just how many could be seen within the city limits. On an area just North of the City, aptly known as Eagle Beach, I was able to study the Bald Eagle at close quarters. I hope in my painting *Low Tide – Bald Eagles* I have captured something of the atmosphere of that day.

Bald
Eagles @
Eagle River, Alaska
May '85

"Low Tide - Bald Eagles"

80

58 *Low Tide – Bald Eagles*
JOHN SEEREY-LESTER (1945–)
Oil on board, 61×91 cm (24×36 in), signed and dated
1986

(a) Preliminary pencil sketch (opposite)
(b) Finished work. This is a very satisfactory
composition, combining a sensible positioning and
proportion between the birds and foreground
driftwood with the distant woods and mountains.
The tidal mud looks really slimy and wet (above)

Having considered together the oil painters of raptors shown at NATURE IN ART, we next look at those who paint other birds.

SIR PETER MARKHAM SCOTT (1909–89) was the only son of the Antarctic explorer, Capt Robert Falcon Scott, who died on his way back from the South Pole in 1911. As he lay dying in his tent while a blizzard raged outside, Capt Scott wrote a last letter to his wife. In it he said of Peter, 'Make the boy interested in natural history if you can: it is better than games; they encourage it at some schools.' Peter's mother, who was an able sculptress, did as her husband suggested.

Sir Peter achieved world recognition as a far-seeing conservationist, interested in all living wild things, as much in whales and coral reef fish as he was in the ducks and geese with which he is more often associated. He was among the first to see the importance of preserving the environment in which endangered species live as the most cost-effective method of preserving the living things themselves. In particular he wrote eloquently of the need to protect the delicately balanced ecosystems of the Antarctic from the ruin that would accompany commercial exploitation of the minerals, fish and other treasures there.

His great contributions to the world as conservationist, artist, broadcaster, Olympic yacht racer and in many other roles, were recognised by Her Majesty the Queen in her award of a Knighthood in 1973 (the first for services to wildlife conservation), and, later, the Companion of Honour and, by the élite of scientists, Fellowship of the Royal Society. A born leader and communicator, he inspired the world to treasure its wildlife long before the 'green' parties got going. He was Founder of the Wildfowl and Wetlands Trust and helped establish the World Wide Fund for Nature (WWF), for which he designed the famous panda logo. Among his many commitments, he was able to be the first President of SWAN from its foundation until his death shortly before his eightieth birthday.

Peter Scott was equally versatile as a painter. The fourth of the thirty published books which he wrote and illustrated was of drawings of human portraits. (A further seventy-eight books or booklets were illustrated in whole or in part by him and eleven others had contributions by him.) He became internationally famous for his paint-ings, nearly always in oil on canvas, particularly those of ducks, swans and geese. He was fortunate in establishing a firm reputation for this as a young man. But later he spread his activities to include whales, fish, moths and much else.

I recognise four phases in the development of his wildlife painting. In the first, largely before 1939, he used a free and vigorous style, often (very convincingly) showing his birds in flight. In the next, from the forties to the sixties, probably because of all the illustrative work that he under-took, he became less 'free' and more detailed in his rendering of birds and background. Some of these paintings, while more accurate from the bird iden-tification and illustrative point of view, were less successful as pictures. Next came a shorter period (the seventies) when he dabbed all the newly applied (and still wet) paint on the canvas with a pad made of his wife's discarded tights. This gave the surface of the painting a prickly appearance and all the images an indistinct edge, making some wonder if their eyesight was suddenly deteriorat-ing. The eighties were typified by much simpler depiction of the birds, often shown almost as silhouettes with back-lighting, as in Plate 59.

A long-time friend, fellow dinghy-sailor and supporter of Peter Scott is KEITH SHACKLETON. Born in 1923 and educated, like Peter, at Oundle School, he served in the Royal Air Force in World War II and subsequently worked until 1963 as a pilot and director of Shackleton Aviation Ltd, a firm founded by his father. 'I could not found a winkle stall,' Keith says! Since then he has had a very distinguished career as an artist. He has been President of the Society of Wildlife Artists and the Royal Society of Marine Artists and Chairman of the Artists' League of Great Britain. He has written and illustrated five books and done paint-ings for many more. In 1986 he was honoured with the Master Wildlife Artist award by the Leigh Yawkey Woodson Art Museum, Wausau, Wis-consin. His twenty years' experience as naturalist to the adventure ship *Lindblad Explorer* in polar seas has given him unique opportunities as an artist. His *Albatross Escort* (Plate 60) reflects his total familiarity with this Antarctic bird and the cold seas which are its home. Commissioned by Shell UK Oil, *Puffins* (Plate 61) was one of four paintings depicting birds of the North Sea after which four Shell oil fields were named.

In his most recent book, *Wildlife and Wilderness: An Artist's World*, he writes with perception and humour of his experiences and sources of inspira-tion. From it he has kindly allowed me to quote:

Of all the ingredients that go to making paint-ers, good or bad, acclaimed or otherwise, the only one that matters is sincerity with oneself and this simply means painting, or trying to paint, from the heart, and doing one's own thing. Influences are bound to raise their heads because people seem to want it, or consciously avoiding something because it is supposedly out of fashion. As sure as tomorrow's dawn will break, opinions of any finished work will cover the whole spectrum from unreserved admira-tion through indifference to vomiting, but if it is sincere it has at least some built-in integrity that can never be denied . . .

If lovely things are important enough, and indeed lovely enough, and the artist feels a desire to pay some sort of homage or tribute, something must be astir. If that person has what Konrad Lorentz describes as 'gestalt-perception', a natural ability to analyse shapes, see shapes within shapes and distil their signifi-cance, things are warming up nicely. Then bringing it all to the boil must surely call for the flame of actual pencilcraft, brushcraft or whatever.

Many, I am sure, would seek to disagree, but to me it seems axiomatic that if you seek to por-tray or interpret something in paint, you need both tools and ability as well as inspiration. I would hesitate to suggest which of the three is the more important, but to miss out on any one would seem like a concert pianist attempting a Chopin sonata with a doughnut in each hand.

All these pictures are oil paintings and I have painted nothing else since childhood. There are sound reasons for being in such a rut and several of them, but much the soundest is that watercolours are too difficult . . . But I just love watercolours – other people's water-colours – to look at. I wish more than anything else that I could handle them. A lot of my friends are watercolourists. I envy all of them and the only consolation I can salvage is that of knowing that I have at least demonstrated the good sense to know when I am licked.

59 *Pintail Pursuit at Sunrise*
PETER MARKHAM SCOTT (1909–89)
Oil on canvas, 90×60 cm (36×24 in), signed and
dated 1987

Typical of the fourth period of his work, with the
birds silhouetted against the sun, this is a study in
the forms and patterns in nature as much as a picture
of pintail landing beside the reeds

84

60 *Albatross Escort*
KEITH SHACKLETON (1923–)
Oil on canvas, 76×101.5 cm (30×40 in), signed and dated 1985

Painted specially for the NATURE IN ART collection, this study admirably captures the effortless ease with which these birds glide for mile after mile over the glistening, deep, cold, restless, antarctic seas

61 *Puffins*
KEITH SHACKLETON (1923–)
Oil on canvas, 46×65 cm (18×25½in), signed and dated 1976

These perky little birds nest in old rabbit burrows on the cliff-tops. They bring from the sea beaks full of sandeels for their chicks and are as deft in catching more fish under the water in a beak that already holds several as they are in manoeuvring in the wind currents around the cliffs

Living on an island in the Baltic Sea as Liljefors (see below) did, LARS JONSSON (see page 67) is familiar with the birds which feed on the seashore. His *Common Gull* (Plate 62) shows his skill in depicting light and form in oils. A creature that is completely white (or black) is as difficult for the artist to portray successfully as it is for the photographer. Here the light on the back of the gull's head casts a shadow over its shoulder and forehead, and under its chest, which together give the bird a convincing three-dimensional look. It looks clean and healthy. Its feathers lie naturally and are not in such ruffled detail as some artists have felt obliged to show, probably because they were painting from dead specimens and were not sufficiently familiar with how sleek and unruffled a really healthy bird looks. The economy in the use of detail (here confined to the eyes and beak), the restraint of the foreground, and the gentle reflection of the bird in the wet mud, all are evidence of his maturity and skill.

Here we turn from paintings of birds to those of mammals, and to six artists, all now dead, from five different European countries and among the most notable painters of wildlife in the last hundred years.

It is difficult to single out one artist, from among so many, as having the greatest impact on the wildlife art world and any such decision will be disputed. However, for me, and for many others, BRUNO LILJEFORS (1860–1939) made a more significant contribution to painting nature than any other individual. He was a man of his time. Growing up with the Darwinian controversy, he accepted that nature could seem harsh, that the fit and the strong survived when the weak did not. He was willing, in his paintings, to show eagles killing prey and foxes hunting theirs. He was both an outdoors man and an astute observer: to him, animals were individuals and he painted them as such. His familiarity with snow and sea scenes

62 *Common Gull and Stones*
LARS JONSSON (1952–)
Oil on canvas, 72×92 cm (28×36 in), signed and dated 1987

The brightness of the sun and the stillness of the day are both well depicted here. Calm water allows brilliant reflections. Successfully painting a black-and-white bird is as difficult as photographing one

made his paintings of these particularly vivid (Plate 63).

Born in Uppsala, Sweden, into a humble home, he lived at first in primitive conditions and was often ill. Probably as a result, he was small in stature. But he was determined to succeed and later set himself daily exercises to improve his physique. This was so successful that he and his brother, Pontus, became members of a Swedish team of gymnasts that toured Europe in 1879.

Liljefors studied at the Royal Academy of Fine Arts in Stockholm. There he shared accommodation with, and was influenced by, his fellow student, Anders Zorn (1860–1920), who was already establishing a reputation by his vigorous landscape paintings. Liljefors described how Zorn broke the accepted painting conventions of the day. By boldly applying colour next to colour in the correct strength to indicate the tonal values of the main features, he created the (false) impression in the viewer's mind that he had painted in detail.

To be nearer the nature he loved, Liljefors moved to live on the Baltic coast in 1890. He was very fortunate in that the critics approved his work depicting nature (a most original and enlightened opinion in those days), even before the public had recognised his skills as a painter. Such was the success of his 1907 exhibition, that he was able to buy an archipelago in the Baltic Sea as his own nature reserve. He was not an illustrator. He did not need to be, even at a time when, in other countries, many able painters, because their paintings were not sufficiently appreciated at the time, were forced to earn their living by illustration. The public response to the work of an artist is as much to do with the prevailing opinions of the critics and academics of the time as with the intrinsic merit of the artist's creations. So the Swedish fine art critics of his day deserve credit for recognising his ability and the genuine validity of his natural subject-matter. If all those in positions of influence in other nations had taken a similar view at that time, wildlife art would now be in a far stronger position.

Martha Hill, in her beautifully illustrated book about Liljefors, *The Peerless Eye*, quotes him on the subject of the inspiration of his work:

Always, when we see something beautiful, inherent in the enjoyment itself is a wish to

share it with someone else. That which gives the wilderness its charm is its unspoilt force and distinctive character, its remoteness from human interference. How then to make this palpable?

WILHELM KUNHERT (1865–1926) was born in Oppeln, Germany, and had his studio in Berlin. Like Liljefors, he was a keen hunter and naturalist. (At that time there did not seem to be any inconsistency in following both pursuits.) As a young man he dreamed of exploring and hunting in East Africa. He made expeditions to what was then German East Africa in 1891, 1905 and 1911 where he witnessed vast numbers of wild animals. He was fortunate to be there before the devastating effects of man's hunting and poaching had appeared. He thus became thoroughly familiar with a wide variety of animals and with the local people. He made portraits of them but the majority of his paintings and drawings were, not surprisingly, of East African animals and birds (Plates 64, 65, 66). He specialised in big cats, so much so that he was sometimes called 'Lowen-Kunhert' (Lion Kunhert). His extended travels enabled him to return with numerous hunting trophies, which later lined the walls of his spacious studio, but the prolonged absences from home finally caused the breakdown of his marriage. After his 1911 tour, he withdrew to his studio at Luitpoldstrasse, Berlin, and worked hard to produce a series of fine, large oil paintings.

The best of his paintings have a freshness of colour and sense of drama, as well as an astute sense of the vivacious spirit in the animal that was his subject (Plate 66). His subjects do not look dead and stuffed, as those of some lesser men have done, no doubt because he had so thoroughly observed living animals while on safari.

An artist, like a prophet, is often not honoured in his own country, at least during his lifetime. Kunhert was not as fortunate as Liljefors. He sold most of his work to private collectors, travellers and big-game hunters who had been to East Africa, rather than to art museums. So it was that he became more famous in England, America and Holland that in his native Germany.

Another German, CARL RUNGIUS (1869–1959) was born in Berlin. He studied art at the Berlin Art School and at the Academy of Fine Arts and

63   *Winter Landscape with Snow Hare*
BRUNO LILJEFORS (1860–1939)
Oil on canvas, 70.5×100.5 cm (27¾×39½ in) signed
and dated 1923

Here is the master at work. The simplicity of
brushwork, the cleanness of colours and the sureness
of composition are typical. The hare momentarily
hesitates to put its paws in the snow mixed with
meltwater

64   *Crowned Crane*
WILHELM KUNHERT (1865–1926)
Pencil sketch, signed and dated 10 Dec 1911
'O. Afrika' (abbreviated German for East Africa)

In addition to the standing and sitting cranes, the
head of an Egyptian goose is also shown

65   *Royal Tiger at the Well*
WILHELM KUNHERT (1865–1926)
Oil on canvas, 100.5×173 cm (39½×68 in)

This large canvas majestically captures the tense
watchfulness of a tiger ready to drink or defend
itself. Detail in the face is sufficient. Brushwork
elsewhere is bold and simple

66   *Waterbuck*
WILHELM KUNHERT (1865–1926)
Oil on canvas, 66.3×90 cm (26×35½ in)

A charming composition, with the subject clearly
shown and the surroundings skilfully unfussed. It
might have been even better if the central rock had
been less prominent and kept below the level of the
animal's nose

67 *Big Horn Sheep in Jasper Park, Rocky Mountains, Alberta, Canada*
CARL RUNGIUS (1869–1959)
Oil on canvas, 76.5×102 cm (30×40 in)

This is a study in nature's patterns and camouflage. The strong diagonal lines of the rock strata distract attention from the (now rare) wild sheep. Much of the colour is applied in blocks, as if the picture was stained glass

began at once to specialise in painting animals. Fortunately for him, this was more acceptable to the critics in Germany at the time than in most other European countries. Like many of his contemporaries, he was both a keen hunter and a wildlife artist. The hunting provided plenty of opportunity to observe wild animals living in their natural habitat and to make himself thoroughly familiar with both the geological structure of the scenery and the appearance of his subjects at a distance, and, after they had been shot, at close quarters (Plates 67, 68).

68 *Mountain Goats, Athabaska, Rocky Mountains, Alberta, Canada*
CARL RUNGIUS (1869–1959)
Oil on canvas, 64×76.5 cm (25×30 in)

Strong diagonal lines here too enhance, rather than spoil, the daring, successful composition and the sense of sun in the foreground and shade in the valley far below

In 1895 he went on a hunting and sketching holiday to Yellowstone Park, in the United States, that initiated a life-long interest in the fauna of the western parts of Canada and the USA. Making his studio in Banff, Canada, his base, he spent the summer camping, hunting, painting and sketching, mostly in the Yukon area, Alberta (Canada) and Wyoming (USA). For the winter he went to his studio in New York City. It was while he was in Banff that he was met by the wildlife artist Francis Lee Jaques (1887–1969) and his wife Florence. She described him as a small man, 'as tough as a pine knot'. When Rungius was in his seventies, he told them that he thought that it was his continued practice of going back-packing that kept him from becoming an old man.

Initially, he had to depend for his living partly on illustrations for outdoor magazines. But in 1912, when the Zoological Society of New York commissioned a series of paintings of North American mammals, he was able to abandon his illustrative work and devote his entire energies to creating gallery-type pictures. For a time he also gave up painting animals in his landscapes and, as a result, had the honour of being elected to membership of the National Academy of Design (which gives a glimpse of the low esteem for wildlife art at that time). After his election, he returned to showing mammals in his oil paintings. A brush was in his hand when he died at the age of ninety.

Intriguing problems arise when making a correct attribution of works of art when they are not signed by the artist. Some famous national collections have been shown in recent years to have forgeries which had been attributed to the masters. NATURE IN ART owns an oil painting of a lion and lioness (Plate 69) by an unknown artist. It was bought in London in 1987 from a German dealer in German paintings. He did not know who had painted the work but said he had bought it from an elderly couple in Germany.

It was Clarence Tillenius (see page 99) who suggested that it might be by GEZA VASTAGH (1866–1919) who was born in what used to be called Klausenberg, more recently Clug-Napoca, in Romania, but lived most of his life in Hungary. He studied under his father George Vastagh, then a well-known Hungarian genre and portrait painter and under Professor Hackl (one of an artistic family of five painters and sculptors) in Munich. Geza Vastagh had his work exhibited widely in Europe, particularly in Munich, London, Paris and Budapest.

In England the Pears Soap Company had established a notable reputation for reproducing a few popular paintings as coloured plates (for removal and framing) in their *Christmas Annual* (1891–1912), including *Bubbles* by Sir John Everett Millais in 1897. What made Geza Vastagh famous in Great Britain was the fact that Pears thus reproduced his painting of the lion and lioness. The original for this painting is signed and dated 1899, even though Vastagh did not always sign his works. At the time of reproduction, the original belonged to Thomas J. Barratt. He had married the daughter of Francis Pears, grandson of the founder of the firm, and was subsequently taken into partnership in charge of marketing and he later became the managing director. The painting was acquired by J. Russell-Cotes, of Bournemouth, who bequeathed it to the town with a large personal collection which is now in the Russell-Cotes Art Gallery and Museum, Bournemouth.

The painting in the NATURE IN ART collection (Plate 69), while similar to the Vastagh original, is not signed and is smaller (52×75cm [20½×29½in] as compared with 94×124cm [37×49in]). The brushwork is less detailed than that in the published Vastagh painting, and there are some distinct, though minor, differences in subject detail between them. So who painted the copy at NATURE IN ART and when and why? Was it a rough, preliminary study made by Vastagh for his larger work or was it a re-working by him of a very successful subject? The difference in brushwork and the colours used make these options improbable. The painting is also unlikely to be the work of a forger because the differences, though minor, are obvious. And if he had done the work deliberately to deceive, the forger surely would also have reproduced the signature.

We have seen two other oil paintings of the same subject, though by much more amateur hands, which suggests that the original reproduced by Pears Soap was so popular that copies of it were made by admirers, amateur and professional. It seems likely that the NATURE IN ART version is such a copy. Thus, to say that it is 'after Geza Vastagh' seems to be a safe assessment.

OTTO PFEIFFER (1882–1955) was born in Mulhouse, then in Germany and now in France, and studied at the École des Beaux-Arts in Strasbourg. In 1907 he married and moved to continue his studies in Vienna and thence, in 1914, to the small town of Haida in Bohemia, then part of Austria-Hungary, now Czechoslovakia. Much of his work was lost, presumably destroyed, during World War II. In 1948, with the Communist takeover, he escaped from Czechoslovakia in a hurry, leaving virtually all his belongings and surviving artwork behind. He settled in France and continued to work there until his death.

Pfeiffer was a versatile artist who painted large canvases and murals, in oils, of wildlife and racehorses for estates now in Poland and Czechoslovakia (Plates 70, 71). His work was exhibited in art galleries and museums in Prague, Dusseldorf, Cologne and Basle. He also designed decoration for engraved crystal glass, both in Haida, Czechoslovakia (said to be the 'capital' of Bohemian glass engraving), and, later, at the Cristallerie Lorraine in France. Pfeiffer's daughter, Mrs Gerth-Pfeiffer, who lives in Amsterdam, has spent many years collecting her father's work and donating or lending the best pieces to museums in Europe (including NATURE IN ART) and the United States of America.

PIETER DIK (1946–84) was born in northern Holland. Like many others described in this book, he showed his artistic interests and skills at an early age and later had some initial difficulty in getting the public to appreciate them. Fortunately, he was willing to live a spartan existence. With travel to Scandinavia, Scotland and North America, after he became a professional artist in 1965, his fine artistic talents began to be recognised. He exhibited his work in at least seven European countries and in North America. Sadly, he died from cancer while he was still young and before he could be more internationally recognised. NATURE IN ART is very fortunate to own two of his works.

His paintings convey the 'atmosphere' of the wild places he loved (Plate 72). He rarely used sketch-books to record what he saw on his expeditions. He either took all his equipment and painted pictures direct in the forest, or he simply absorbed into his acute memory the scenes he saw and recreated their atmosphere onto canvas in his

69   *Lion and Lioness*
After GEZA VASTAGH (1866–1919)
Oil on canvas, 52×75 cm (20½×29½ in)

The brushwork is skilful in that there is no attempt
at fussy detail. Both look tiredly content. For
attribution see text

(Opposite)
72 *The Sounder – Wild Boar*
PIETER DIK (1943–84)
Oil on canvas, 83×68 cm (32¾×26¾ in)

By priming the whole canvas with pale blue paint, he
has already done a third of the picture – sky and
foreground need little more work on them! With his
usual skill and simple brushwork, he has shown both
the atmosphere of the forest and the golden-striped
young boars

70 *Greater-spotted Woodpeckers*
OTTO PFEIFFER (1882–1955)
Oil on board, 27×20.5 cm (10½×8 in), signed and
dated 1935

Textures, light and shade and composition are
handled well in this little painting

(Right)
71 *Polish Forest and Red Deer*
OTTO PFEIFFER (1882–1955)
Oil on canvas, 39×49.5 cm (15½×19½ in)

Preliminary sketch for one of four very large murals
in a baronial castle in Poland. The 'atmosphere' of
the scene is the main subject and is skilfully handled.
The stag and his hind are dwarfed by the huge
conifers. Beyond the clearing the forest is dark. The
distant vista is vital to the composition, inviting
exploration and preventing claustrophobia

studio. Free brushwork (eg foreground, Plate 73) is characteristic of his work. The minimum detail is economically applied where it is essential, such as the head of the animal or bird that he depicts, and is scrupulously avoided where the human eye could not see it, such as the rapidly moving wings of the woodcock (Plate 73).

Next, we consider leaders among living wildlife artists who depict mammals (among other subjects). The distinction is somewhat artificial, I confess, because painters like Robert Bateman, Raymond Harris-Ching and John Seerey-Lester

73 Woodcock Roding
PIETER DIK (1943–84)
Oil on canvas, 85×71 cm (33½×28 in)

Free brushwork and the quiet colours of nature are here skilfully used to create this evocative scene. Look closely at how he has applied his paint

are equally at ease showing birds and mammals. None the less, this grouping enables some interesting comparisons to be made.

CLARENCE TILLENIUS, born of Scandinavian parents in Manitoba, Canada, in 1913, has spent his whole working life drawing and painting the wild creatures of northern Canada. Years of travelling with Indians and the Inuit people of the Canadian north gave him total familiarity with the wildlife in those wilderness areas. His palette may seem strange to those who have never seen the prairies under snow or the pack-ice off Baffin Island, but to those who know them, the colours he uses for his vigorous oil sketches (Plate 74) and gallery pictures (Plate 75) are correct.

The loss of his right arm in a construction accident in 1936 could have cost him his painting career. But not so. Undaunted, he studied under a fine artist and great friend, Alexander Musgrove, while perfecting the use of his left hand. It is

74 Ridge-bordered Marsh
CLARENCE TILLENIUS (1913–)
Field sketch, oil on board, 24×50.5 cm (9½×20 in), signed and dated 1988

As he often does, Tillenius here almost conceals one of the two animals, while the smaller one is silhouetted against the winter reeds. This painting has all the realism and freshness of an on-site painting. It had to be made quickly because of the very low temperature

essential to remember this when one reads of his astonishing travels in the Arctic. His modest descriptions of the difficulty and danger of trying to draw or paint, or even take a photograph, when the temperature can be −50°C take on a new significance.

His travels, painting, writing and lecturing led to his election as an International Fellow of the prestigious Explorers' Club in New York. He is a

75 *Prairie Creek in Winter – Jack Rabbits Foraging*
CLARENCE TILLENIUS (1913–)
Oil on canvas, 41×61 cm (16×24 in), signed and
dated 1983

The great cold of the vast, flat prairies of northern
Canada, the drifts of crisp snow, the clear light and
surprisingly bright colours are all successfully
captured in this scene

Founding Member of the Society of Animal Artists of New York and has won important distinctions and awards including an Honorary Doctorate of Law from the University of Winnipeg (1970). As Francis Lee Jaques (1887–1969) had done in the United States, Tillenius has created dioramas for the major museums across Canada. Tillenius writes:

Art that is to endure must always derive its strength from nature; that is, the artist must have a profound understanding of, and feeling for, the elemental sources of things, the rhythms of life that are not affected by passing fashions. In my paintings of animals and wilderness, I strive to convey what I feel about these things, to portray a wilderness world intelligible to any human being who is exhilarated by a mountain sunrise, who sees with pleasure a rabbit track across a snowy field, or who simply enjoys being outdoors. It is wrong to think that the viewer of a painting must be a connoisseur of art, or even must know how the painting was done. It is the business of the artist to perfect a technique that will communicate what he feels about what he chooses to paint.

DAVID SHEPHERD was born in England in 1931. He refers to his early life as 'a series of disasters'. While a boy at school it was his ambition to become a game warden in East Africa. When he left Stowe School, he went to Kenya in 1950 'with the arrogant assumption that I was God's gift to the Kenya National Parks'. He was not appointed and came home again with his 'world in ruins'. He then decided that he would somehow pursue his only other interest, art. He applied to the Slade School of Art but was turned down as 'not worth teaching'. 'That was the best thing that ever happened to me,' he told me. By good fortune he met the marine artist Robin Goodwin who took him on as a full-time student from 1950 to 1953. David attributes all his success to Goodwin. 'I had no talent whatsoever – Robin could have taught anybody to paint.'

At first, David specialised in one of his first loves, aviation. In 1960 he was invited to Aden and Kenya in connection with commissioned work for the Royal Air Force. While he was there he gained his first commission to paint a wildlife picture: for the Royal Air Force Officers' Mess in Nairobi. His reputation as an animal painter grew rapidly after his first one-man exhibition at the Tryon Gallery, London, in 1962. Since then he has had many other, equally successful, exhibitions in Europe, Africa and the United States. Several television programmes have been made about his life and work and his interest in wildlife conservation. He has also had five successful books published, including *David Shepherd: The Man and His Paintings* (1985).

In spite of his international reputation for wildlife paintings, he has never completely given up painting scenes from aviation history or steam railways which are his other main interest. Indeed, it was through the success of his wildlife paintings that he was able to buy two giant steam locomotives from British Rail and he is the Founder of the East Somerset Railway, a registered charity, which also helps to raise funds for wildlife conservation. In addition, he has found time to paint portraits of, among others, Her Majesty Queen Elizabeth, the Queen Mother, and His Excellency Dr Kenneth Kaunda, President of Zambia.

David says that he owes all his success to the wildlife that he paints and, because of this and the fact that he has had many first-hand experiences of the horrors of what man has done to the environment, he is 'now passionately involved with the conservation of wildlife'. He has formed his own charity, the David Shepherd Conservation Foundation. He says that 'the greatest reward in my life is to be able to return the debt I owe to wildlife and also to those who have helped me in my career'.

Perhaps his most famous painting was *Tiger Fire*, painted in 1973 to help save the tiger from the brink of extinction. Through the donation of the painting and the sale of prints, this raised over £125,000 for Project Tiger in India. Furthermore, because it was the RAF who took him back to Africa and started him on his career of wildlife painting, he donated to the RAF Benevolent Fund the entire print edition of his painting of a Lancaster bomber, *Winter '43, Somewhere in England*, and thereby raised more than £95,000. He generously gave the original painting shown in Plate 76 to NATURE IN ART. Altogether, he has now raised 'somewhere in the region of two million pounds' for charitable purposes. 'The more I learn of what

man is doing, the more determined I am to repay my debt to wildlife.' In recognition of his work for wildlife conservation he was awarded the Order of the British Empire (1975). He has also been awarded the Order of the Golden Ark by Prince Bernhard of the Netherlands, been elected a Fellow of the Royal Society of Arts and has been elected an Honorary Doctor of Fine Arts at the Pratt Institute, New York.

Another painter of East African big game is SIMON COMBES. He was born in England in 1940 but emigrated with his parents, brother and grandmother to Kenya when he was aged six. Here he grew up among the animals he learned to love and respect. In his book *An African Experience. Wildlife Art and Adventure in Kenya*, he gives a vivid, amusing and fascinating account of his varied life at two schools, his expeditions with a rifle out in the wild country under the care of local tribesmen, his early zeal for shooting big game and then his turn from it, in his mid-twenties, to painting and drawing the animals he used to kill, his career as a white man in the Kenyan Army and his decision to become a professional painter.

Associated with each of the sixty-seven coloured reproductions of his oil paintings, is an eloquent commentary on the scene: interesting facts about its subject and thoughts on the technique and motive in the creation of the painting. For example, of *A Quail Quails*, Simon Combes asks:

How many times does one wish that certain split-second moments in time could be frozen for posterity? The great privilege of a painter or photographer is to be able to achieve that and many of my paintings strive to that end.

Here is an example. A serval cat poised motionless, straining every one of its senses to pinpoint the quail which crouches under the tussock of grass. The quail has three options – run, fly or freeze. Natural instinct will dictate which to choose but any of them are fraught with danger. The cat also expects any of the three and readies itself to react accordingly – chase, swipe or pounce.

The trick is to set the scene for potential action and leave the viewer to speculate on the outcome.

76 *The Three Old Gentlemen of Savuti*
DAVID SHEPHERD (1931–)
Oil on canvas, 71×155 cm (28×61 in), signed and dated Jan 1990

Painted specially for the NATURE IN ART collection, this typifies David's recent work. The dominance of the central bull is the essence of the picture. David comments 'Savuti is the most marvellously exciting piece of Africa near the Okavango swamps in Botswana'

77 *Savannah Elephants*
SIMON COMBES (1940–)
Oil on canvas, 122×244 cm (48×96 in), signed and
dated Sept 1989

Pencil sketches:
(a) First idea (above)
(b) Revised version (opposite above)
(c) Second revision (opposite below)
(d) Finished work (overleaf). Both terrain and
animals are shown in some detail. The dead tree and
the egrets on the earth mound were included to
improve the composition and add interest

In a personal note about *Savanna Elephants* (Plates
77a, b, c, d), Simon Combes says:

About a quarter of the total time taken on any
one painting is devoted to what I call prepara-
tion; in other words everything before the first
brush stroke is made on the canvas. To my mind
this is the most critical phase . . .

Having acquired a mental image of my
intended subject, I spend many hours doodling
in a sketch pad, trying to transfer my idea to
paper and work out a composition in its
simplest form. Throughout this process I pull
out hundreds of photographs to provide sup-
plementary ideas such as skies, trees, light
effects, grass, rocks and indeed the animal
itself. As the days go by, the chaos in my studio
increases until it is barely possible to move
about for fear of treading on photos, sketches
and books . . . During this painful period I
become increasingly introverted, monosyllabic
and a pain in the neck to the rest of the family.
At last, and hopefully after not too long, I can
go firm on a composition and really start to
develop a working drawing . . . I think composition is largely instinctive and something that I
will never cease to learn about or be frustrated
with . . . It is crucial to establish one's light
source at the very beginning . . .

I am often asked whether I try to make some
kind of statement through my paintings. It
always amuses me that, because you paint,
people imagine you as being on some higher
intellectual plane ready to trot out highly aes-
thetic and quotable statements. Not so in my
case. I love Africa; I love animals; I am more
than fortunate to be able to paint these two
obsessions and it gives me much pleasure and
satisfaction if I can share them, through my
work, with other people.

One of the challenges facing a painter is the desirability but difficulty of creating, in a static two-dimensional painting, the impression of movement. There are various devices which an artist employs to achieve this. In *Cougar Run* (Plate 78), John Seerey-Lester (see page 80) makes the large wild North American cat seem to be leaping towards the viewer. This impression is made, in addition to the posture of the cougar, by the detailed painting of the animal's fur, particularly around its eyes and face, and partly by the slightly exaggerated size of the front paws and the flying snow they have displaced.

78   *Cougar Run*
JOHN SEEREY-LESTER (1945–)
Acrylic on board, 91.5×91.5 cm (37×36 in), signed and dated 1989

(a) Preliminary pencil sketch. A colour sketch (not shown) depicted the big cat in a hot grassland scene (b) Finished work (opposite). The gentleness of the background contrasts with the powerful pounce of the cat. It might have appeared even more striking if the rocks did not project above its head

Careful depiction of fur and skin folds, the eyes and noses of tigers at rest, is the key to the success of *White Tigers Ever Watchful* (Plates 79a, b) by ANTHONY GIBBS. Here too the posture of the head and the position of the feet, restfully following the contours of the uneven ground, are crucial to the success of the painting. The preliminary sketches (Plate 79a) show how Gibbs has concentrated his attention (consciously or unconsciously) on these features. He writes:

I had the idea for a painting of a white tiger two or three years before I painted it. I thought it would be a good idea because I didn't think anyone else had painted a white tiger up to that time.

I went to the Bristol Zoo in March 1986 to see and photograph the white tiger there. The tiger on the left in my painting is this tiger.

I heard it had died a month later. It was such a beautiful cat and I was so sad to hear it had died I felt I had to start the painting straight away. It took fifteen weeks to complete. I spent two weeks on the leaves alone. It was worth it.

Anthony Gibbs was born in Birmingham, England, in 1951 and studied at the Bourneville School of Art. His first one-man exhibition was in Birmingham and he has since had others there, all equally successful. He specialises in landscapes and wildlife.

If an artist can successfully and convincingly depict the eyes and feet of his subject, he will virtually be bound to make at least a technical success of the whole painting. But getting the eye slightly the wrong size or shape or just out of the strictly correct position is all too easy. Some artists tend to make the eye too big which gives it a sentimental appearance. Others make the legs too long, thin, squat or whatever, or put them in a position where they cannot possibly support the creature, which seems to be particularly a problem when depicting birds. Many artists have thus exposed themselves to criticism from an increasingly knowledgeable and discerning public. Some viewers may not be able to say what is wrong with a picture but they are instinctively dissatisfied with it.

79 *White Tigers Ever Watchful*
ANTHONY GIBBS (1951–)
Oil on canvas, 76×152 cm (30×60 in)

(a) Preliminary pencil sketch (opposite)
(b) Finished work. Even though the artist never saw this scene, he has contrived a successful composition without falling into the many potential pitfalls of an imaginary setting. The faces are particularly successfully depicted (above)

RAYMOND HARRIS-CHING (see also page 50) was born in Wellington, New Zealand, in 1939. He first attracted attention as a portrait painter and did not begin to paint birds until he was twenty-four. He has illustrated six very successful books, four of which are specifically about him and his art, including *The Art of Raymond Ching* (1981). In 1967 he made England his base from which he travels the world.

He has made his reputation through both his books and his accurate draughtsmanship. His artistry lies in skilful picture composition, often combined with restraint and simplicity in the background of many of his (particularly recent) paintings. Having worked mostly in watercolours, he now usually uses oil colours on board, or occasionally canvas. For his subjects, he has given more attention than most artists to the humbler birds and beasts, in Europe and Australia. He says, 'Making something wonderful on canvas from a sparrow is to me much more satisfactory than a merely successful peacock.' The kangaroo (Plate 80) is an animal largely ignored by artists so far. The detailed parts of the picture are cleverly and economically distributed. Of this painting, he writes:

A male red kangaroo stands in a swirl of red dust as three pink cockatoos, frightened by the storm, flutter about to gain a perch on its back. A few sticks and dry leaves flick about in the heat, while the kangaroo is defined quite sculpturally, central in the painting, with a deep illusion of space before and behind.

It seemed necessary to me that the animal be painted as more than just itself . . . it must, of course, be true to its own self (indeed, my painting followed most closely the many drawings I had made of this animal) but I felt it just as important to transcend its natural history.

I wanted this young male kangaroo to represent, not so much its species, as the land itself, with all its vulnerability – a land that can, at any moment be swept into disaster. Inextricably tied to the volatile amalgam of flood and fire that is Australia – continuously threatened and constantly regenerating – the animal is seen as an icon of the deep connection that Australians have to their great continent.

Peter Hansard (1988), describing in *Wild Portraits* the recent work of Harris-Ching executed in oils, says:

Ray's painting technique is very much confined to the task of 'drawing' the paint on, so that, for example, bold washes of colour are almost never used.

The form, texture and 'light' are 'drawn' with the brush in rapid strokes very much like those that might be made with a pencil. Normally, Ray begins with what seems a remarkably detailed and complete drawing carried out on a finely sanded and smoothly gessoed panel . . .

Pigment is applied sparingly, always well thinned so that the actual stroke of paint goes on as a more or less transparent mark. The painting is gradually built up in this way, often with pencil lines and underlying coats of gesso still visible even in finished areas. To Ray this 'thinness' is of great importance, it's what he strives for most . . .

Now we look at two artists who use acrylics to depict flowers and, in the second case, insects also.

ROSALIND WISE was born in South Wales in 1949. She studied Fine Art at Reading University from 1968 to 1972. At that time the department had strong inclinations towards abstract art. Of Plate 81 she writes:

I felt very alien from its priorities . . . abstract form for its own sake held little relevance for me, but I completed the course and gained my degree . . . It wasn't until I had left Reading that I began again to draw from nature and feel more at peace with myself and the purpose of my work.

Nature has always been my main source of inspiration. The colour, shapes, patterns and designs in plant form have always held an endless fascination.

I moved to Gloucestershire in 1981, having spent the previous three years teaching in London. During that time I saved enough to have a year off . . . and at last I had time to devote all my energy to studying the plant life around me . . . Each day I would gather specimens and paint them. It was marvellous to watch plants grow, to observe the woodland floor for changes, to lose oneself in looking, to feed oneself on the endless variety there is and to feel humble before all one surveys . . .

I slowly realised that I wanted to paint not just botanical illustrations for their own sake, but for my work to hold a more symbolic significance. The idea of two large canvases showing my concerns emerged, one showing a cycle of a year of flowers, the other a year full of various aspects of trees . . . For the flower canvas I drew a large free-hand spiral from the centre of the canvas outwards. I wanted the painting to represent a year of floral growth beginning at the centre of the canvas with the snowdrop, which for me is symbolic of the end of winter – the beginning of spring, and then to paint each flower as it appears through the year, reaching the autumn at the outside of the canvas. It contains both garden and wild flowers . . . almost two hundred different types.

80 *Eye of the Storm*
RAYMOND HARRIS-CHING (1939–)
Oil on board, 91.5×119 cm (36×47 in), signed and dated 1988

This daring composition succeeds because the bird close to the left edge of the scene keeps the eye from following the kangaroo's tail out of the picture. The artist has painted other pictures with an unusual format

114

82 *Bramble Patch* (preliminary sketches)
RICHARD TRATT (1953–)
Acrylic on paper, 18×43 cm (7×17 in)

Here are field sketches as charming as they are
obviously genuine. Not all so-called preliminary
sketches were done before the finished work! Careful
notes record details, such as the direction of the light

RICHARD TRATT was born in London in 1953. As
a child he drew butterflies and moths with crayons
and this fascination stayed with him. Having
studied at Northwich College of Art, Cheshire,
and Darlington College of Arts, Devon (1970–4),
he is now a full-time artist-naturalist, specialising
in butterflies, moths and flowers. Most of his
paintings are in acrylic on canvas. Of Plates 82 and
83, Richard writes:

Bramble Patch was inspired by a visit to
Bookham Common, Surrey, where the woodland glades provide an ideal haunt for the magnificent Silver Washed Fritillary. In late July
and August the brambles at the glade edge are
amass with butterflies.

My first wildlife paintings were individual
studies of insects and birds. A lifelong interest
in natural history had led me to detailed knowledge of habitats. Fortunately I'd been working
as a landscape painter for many years and gradually was able to merge these two abilities to
produce much larger habitat paintings of actual
places.

I work from field sketches and notes. From
these I make preparatory colour sketches
before embarking on the final work – which is
painted in the studio. Recently I've moved
toward impressionist landscape which I'm able
to paint outdoors so only the finer foreground
details have to be studio painted.

81 *The Cycle of Flowers*
ROSALIND WISE (1949–)
Acrylic on canvas, 241×2,44 cm (84×96 in)

A riot of colour and forms, this large picture begins
at the centre with the snowdrops and celandines of
spring and spirals out to the golden rod, wild carrot
etc of autumn

Last but not least in this chapter, we consider pastels, which are neither watercolours nor oils. Sticks of dry, very finely powdered pigment are bound with a variety of gums or oils. They tend to leave a dusty surface on the paper until it has been 'fixed' with a thin varnish spray. Some pastels can be mixed or diluted with turpentine and others with water. Essentially their use is a form of drawing rather than painting, but the two techniques merge to become inseparable in the hands of most artists who use this difficult medium.

DEBORAH CAMERO was born in New England in 1942 and now lives in the state of Pennsylvania. She studied at Philadelphia College of Art and, privately, under Jacques Fabert and William A. Smith. Of her *Sheltering Wild Ponies – Assateague* (Plates 84a, b), she writes:

To me inspiration is intangible . . . it just happens to me, comes from somewhere I don't know . . . It is all very strange, it can come upon me as I walk the edge of a barrier island, wild and windy and alone or on a crowded street in London. Similarly, music can cause me to want to create a mood or feeling. I will 'see' an image of sorts in my mind; sometimes almost the whole painting I may eventually create. Other times just bits and pieces of a painting, many vague ideas will flow quickly and wildly and I know that I MUST paint that . . .

Sheltering . . . Assateague began with my visit to the barrier island off the coast of Virginia, called Assateague . . . After hours of searching we found several [wild ponies] huddled together waiting out the winds. It was then and there with the sand, sea spray and wind smacking against my face that the 'feeling', the 'inspiration' seized me and I knew I *had* to capture and create that visual mood and make it so that

the viewer could feel he was there. From that moment the painting began to evolve with months of sketching, research, reworked sketches, torn up sketches, more research and more sketches until it 'spoke' to me.

That is the hardest part . . . getting to that point of being ready to paint the final idea. I spend as much time, if not more, researching a painting than painting it. I don't paint by guess or approximation – I take great pains to study the anatomical structure of the animals I draw or paint . . .

Then I begin the art . . . I most often use a French paper made of 100% rag and begin by constructing a very accurate drawing in graphite pencil or pastel pencil. At this stage I begin setting the values with underglazes of color. I strive for luminosity of color, which is why I use a series of glazes and underlayers . . . Whilst applying the underglazes I establish cool areas and middle value areas and warms; as I consider color perspective equally important as linear perspective.

84   *Sheltering Wild Ponies – Assateague*
DEBORAH CAMERO (1942–)
Pastels on paper, 48×61 cm (19×24 in), signed and dated 1987

(a) Preliminary watercolour sketch
(b) Finished work (overleaf). Anyone who has stood on sand-dunes and experienced the wind from the Atlantic on a dull day will almost feel this atmospheric scene and sympathise with the ponies

83   *Bramble Patch*
RICHARD TRATT (1953–)
Acrylic on board, 61×76 cm (24×30 in), signed and dated 1984

The combination of free brushwork and restraint in the depiction of four different types of butterfly, together with dramatic lighting and skilful composition, makes this a charming picture. The simplicity of the painting of the shaded wood is important

PRINTS AND BATIK

Elegant and accurate figures do much illustrate and facilitate the understanding of Descriptions.

Francis Willughby and John Ray,
ORNITHOLOGIA (1676)

A clear definition of the subject of this chapter is particularly important because the term 'print' is so commonly used in widely differing senses. Here, prints are multiple original works of art created by a printing technique from engraved plates, wood blocks, lithographic stones, lino cuts and the like. A feature common to these is the fact that at least part of the final print has been made by hand – in the making of the plate and/or in the colouring of the print from it. But there are some important differences too. In some techniques the print is produced by depressions or grooves in the plate which retain the ink (eg engraving, etching and its variants, aquatint etc). These form an image called an 'intaglio print'. Other methods employ the opposite effect, where it is the uncut surface of the block or plate that transfers the ink to the paper to produce a 'relief print' (eg wood engravings, woodcuts and linocuts). A third type of print is produced with an entirely flat surface ('surface print') by lithography where the distribution of the ink is determined by using a greasy ink and a greasy image on a grease-resisting background. Most museums do not keep and exhibit reproductions entirely produced mechanically, whether signed by the artist or not.

For all the beauty and fascination of watercolours and oil paintings, prints have a charm and interest of their own. Many skills were (and are still) used in their production, varying, of course, according to the type of print. First the design had to be created, often by a preliminary drawing or painting. Then it was transferred onto the plate or block from which the impressions were printed. Because the plate or block was a 'negative', the image had to be the mirror image of the one intended for final viewing.

Where multicoloured pictures were printed, there had to be several different wood blocks, metal plates or lithographic stones, each exactly matching, and aligned ('registered') with, the others. The actual printing required technical skills of a very different kind to the making of the original design, which is why some artists used an expert to make their engravings for them. In the last century and earlier, the final stage of monochrome printing was the hand colouring of thousands of prints. Many artists of the eighteenth and nineteenth centuries had the loyal help of their wives and daughters at this final stage, even though some of them were reluctant to admit it.

Most early prints were intended as illustrations for books. Their purpose was both to convey factual information clearly and to make the book more attractive to read. But many of those who drew the initial pictures from which they themselves, or experts, made the prints, were not only illustrators but gifted artists. Instinctively they often produced genuine works of art as well as information-transmitting illustrations.

An illustration was most likely to be successful if it was made by the artist who knew exactly what he wanted to illustrate, rather than by another etcher or engraver, however skilled he might be. So artists learned to produce their own prints, usually (since they were the techniques most easily mastered) by etching and later by lithography.

An etching was made on a metal plate, usually copper or zinc, coated with a layer of acid-resisting material, such as wax. This was often blackened by a candle flame to make the design scratched in the wax more easily visible. The plate was then immersed in acid and the exposed metal parts were dissolved (or 'bitten') away, while the wax-coated parts remained protected. The strength of colour was determined by the depth, width and spacing of the etched lines. The wider and deeper they were, the more ink they retained and the blacker the image they produced.

A variation of etching technique was called aquatint where the plate was covered with a layer of porous wax which had minute holes in it. These created numerous tiny rings and dots, best seen in the lightly shaded parts of the picture, in contrast with the thin lines of an ordinary etching. Study of a print with a hand lens usually shows which technique was employed.

Engravings, on the other hand, were produced by directly gouging a groove in polished metal with a graver (or burin). This cut lines with sharper edges and ends than those produced by etching. In both cases, it was the grooves created in the plate that held the ink and transferred the image to the paper when it was pressed onto the plate in the printing. We begin by considering the group of intaglio prints, considering etchings, aquatints and engravings together, and grouping them according to their subject-matter so that one artist can more easily be compared with another.

ELEAZER ALBIN (died 1741 or 1742), a professional painter in watercolours, wrote and illustrated *A Natural History of Birds* (1731–8). The illustrations were hand-coloured copper-plate etchings (Plate 85), each depicting one large or two or more smaller birds. The year and place of Albin's birth are unknown. He worked in London, living with his large family first in Soho and later St Pancras. His first book, on English insects, was published in 1714. He liked to depict insects, plants and birds because of their beautiful colouring. He was primarily an artist, but also an amateur naturalist. He became an author in order to give his artwork a wider circulation and thus increase his income.

The long title of his book includes the words 'engraven from the Life . . . from the Originals, Drawn from the Live Birds'. This does not mean what we would think today. Although he had observed some of his subjects in the field (but before the days of binoculars) and also had a few live, caged specimens to draw, most of the paintings were made from dead specimens. This curious practice was later copied by other artists, such as

9

The great Horn Owl Cock

Catesby (see below). Thus 'from the life . . .' means from a specimen rather than from the recollection or imagination of the artist himself or from copying the work of another. (When hard facts were in short supply, there had been no shortage of invention in earlier illustrations.)

Some of the prints in Volumes 1 and 3 were signed 'E. Albin'. It is not certainly known whether these were the work of Eleazar (as has often been assumed) or of his daughter Elizabeth. She signed forty-one of the illustrations in Volume 1 and also assisted with the final colouring of the prints. Whether any of the 306 etchings were made by Albin himself is not known.

Albin's book was the first British book on birds published with coloured illustrations. The first book of the birds of North America was by a fellow Englishman, MARK CATESBY (1683–1749), who was born, educated and lived in England, although it is with America that he is commonly associated. The son of a prosperous landlord and lawyer, he grew up in the Essex countryside and became an accomplished naturalist, encouraged in this by a near neighbour, the renowned naturalist-author John Ray.

In 1712, when Catesby was twenty-nine, he visited his married sister, Elizabeth, in Williamsburg, Virginia. Including a stay in the West Indies, he was in America for seven years before returning to England. During his time there he accumulated a fine botanical collection and sent many specimens back to England. These had attracted the attention of botanists, particularly William Sherard, a Fellow of the Royal Society and a friend of John Ray. Catesby was financed to return to Carolina, early in 1722, on a plant-collecting expedition sponsored by the Royal Society. Based at Charleston, Catesby spent four years collecting plants, mammals, birds, fishes and snakes. He sent barrels full of specimens, some preserved in rum, back to England but prudently he kept careful

85   *The Great Horn Owl Cock*
ELEAZER ALBIN (*d* 1741/2)
Hand-coloured copper-plate etching, 26.5 × 20.5 cm (10½ × 8 in)

To those familiar with this North American bird, it will be clear that the artist has got his colours wrong and not succeeded in much of a likeness. But he certainly has created a character!

drawings and paintings of them in case they failed to complete the hazardous journey.

In 1726 he returned to England and spent the next seventeen years completing *The Natural History of Carolina, Florida and the Bahama Islands . . .* (1731–43), the first book on the fauna and flora of America. He personally made the etchings for all the 220 plates and hand coloured many of them himself. He had help with the colouring as the publication proceeded but assured readers that this was always under his supervision. The work, like so many for the next hundred years or more, was published in parts and subsequently bound into volumes by the subscribers.

We saw, in Chapter 2, that artists in the eighteenth century gradually began to show background in addition to portraits of the subjects themselves. Catesby was one of the pioneers of this idea. His first eight plates had no background at all; the ninth showed a bird on a branch with leaves and fruit, and all the remaining plates attempted to indicate something of the habitat. However, it seems probable that the main reason for this was stimulated not so much by a concern for biological accuracy as by economic expediency! It would have taken him too long to make separate plates to show all the plants, birds, insects etc that he intended, so he combined several on one plate (Plate 86). However, the birds, insects, plants etc were not always shown to the same scale and no indication of life size was given in the plates. Because he initiated the printing of a size larger than was then usual, he was able to depict many of the smaller species life size.

Unlike Albin, Catesby was a field naturalist and made nearly all the original observations that formed the basis of the text that accompanied his coloured plates. Migration, feeding habits and many other details were described for the first time. It was in recognition of the quality of his work in America, and the publication of the first volume of his book (1731), that Catesby was elected a Fellow of the Royal Society in 1733. His work soon came to be appreciated abroad as well. Plate 86 shows one of 747 hand-coloured plates from the first edition of a major work, describing 426 strange and uncommon birds, written in German, engraved, coloured and published (1749–76) by Johann Michael Seligmann (1720–62) after prints by Mark Catesby and George Edwards.

Tab. XXX.   Der blaue Häher.

Similax laevis Lauri folio bacca nigra.

PICA Glandaria caerulea cristata. 30.   GEAI bleu.

GEORGE EDWARDS (1694–1773) was born in the countryside of Essex and, after local schooling, was sent by his father for a seven-year apprenticeship with a bookkeeper and accountant in London. This, it was hoped, would ensure him a prosperous career in business. But the young George had other ideas. Two years after he had finished his apprenticeship, at the age of twenty-four, he set out on an exploration of European countries. He made several visits, including one to Norway, all the time studying natural history and making drawings of what he saw, particularly birds.

In 1733 he was very fortunate to be offered the posts in London of Librarian of the Royal College of Physicians and secretary to Sir Hans Sloane, who was President of the College of Physicians and of the Royal Society at the time. Sir Hans also employed him to draw specimens in his own private collection. Edwards said that other 'curious gentlemen' (we would say, cultured) also brought him specimens to be drawn. He was, as he wrote later, careful to keep copies of all the paintings he

86   *Blue Jay*
After MARK CATESBY (1683–1749)
Hand-coloured copper-plate etching by Johann Michael Seligmann (1720–62), 23×31 cm (9×12 in)

This is one of the most popular of the plates by Catesby. He skilfully combines a named plant and the bird in one pleasing composition – a much more convincing perch than Albin's in Plate 85

did. Over some twenty years he accumulated a fine collection of rarities, many of them unrecorded species. Even though, as he candidly admitted, he knew little or nothing of the habitat of the birds, or even their country of origin, he was persuaded to publish his paintings (Plates 87, 88) in a book, *A Natural History of Uncommon Birds* (1743–51). When all the parts had been published, they were bound into four volumes.

Unlike other artist-authors of his time, he included at the end of his last volume a description of how he etched the copper plates, sometimes with the addition of finishing touches of engraving. He was taught how to make his own etchings

by his friend Mark Catesby. He records how to trace the design onto the plate and draw the design through the protective wax coat on the metal. Rather than immerse the plate, as tradition decreed, he preferred to pour the nitric acid onto the plate. Lighter parts were 'stopped out' with varnish, before further etching to make other areas more deeply 'bitten'.

Edwards was given many honours. He was awarded the prestigious gold Copley medal by the Royal Society. He was elected a Fellow of the Society of Antiquaries in 1733 and of the Royal Society in 1757. Since many think of the FRS as the highest honour in the world of science and the FSA as the best in the arts, to receive both was tribute indeed. Like Catesby, his fame spread to Europe and his work was copied by Seligmann (see page 121) and other authors.

The next milestone in art depicting natural history came from America but was the work of a man born in Paisley, Scotland. ALEXANDER WILSON (1766–1813) was the son of Alexander senior, an ex-smuggler. He became one of the prosperous weavers in the town that made the Paisley silk materials that were so fashionable at that time. Alexander junior was educated at the grammar school and began training for the ministry of the church. But times became hard for him following his mother's death from tuberculosis.

In 1794 Wilson emigrated to America. Failing to get work as a weaver, he found employment in a firm of engravers in Philadelphia and then as a schoolmaster. His own schooling had been so poor that he had to teach himself before he could teach the pupils, a commitment which became a grow-

87 *Blue Jay*
GEORGE EDWARDS (1694–1773)
Hand-coloured copper etching, 24.5×19.5 cm
(9½×7½ in)

This blue jay, from the West Indies, is not meant to be the same as that from North America (Plate 86)

88 *Blue Jay*
GEORGE EDWARDS (1694–1773),
detail from 87

'Bigness of life' = life size. The style of etching and the fact that each plate is signed with a specific day, month and year, is typical of Edwards

ing burden. At the same time he came, increasingly, to appreciate the solitude of the wilderness areas and the lovely birds that seemed to be everywhere. His neighbours were not interested in wildlife, even though folklore relating to it abounded. The only person to encourage him in his studies of nature was William Bartram, the naturalist and botanical painter, of Philadelphia. Wilson's school work prevented much daytime study so at night he made sketches and drawings by candle-light. Finding it easier to make realistic paintings from living creatures, his students brought him a great variety of birds and animals, for which he paid 10 cents each. Some of these became his pets. Wilson's drawing improved rapidly.

Probably helped by his earlier experience soon after his arrival in America and using tools borrowed from an engraver friend in Philadelphia, Alexander Lawson (1773–1846), Wilson taught himself to make engravings of his drawings and made some encouragingly successful prints from them. In 1804 he became a citizen of the United States and marked the occasion by writing one of his many poems. In the same year he first approached a publisher with the idea of writing and illustrating a book about all the birds of that part of America. He was told he was crazy but he knew he was not. He tried to give up his teaching post but the trustees discouraged this by increasing his pay. After he had decided to continue to teach, the sons of Samuel Bradford, an important publisher from Philadelphia, became his pupils.

In 1806 he finally gave up his teaching and took the post of assistant editor of an encyclopaedia to be published in Philadelphia by Bradford. After that events moved fast. In April 1807 the printed prospectus for his ten-volume book *American Ornithology*, with ten coloured plates in each volume, was issued by Bradford. Each plate included between two and four birds. Wilson's ambitious scheme then was to write and illustrate, in colour, a book to describe all North American birds, not just those of the eastern part as he had originally planned. To achieve this, he had to write the text from his own observations, make all the original drawings and colour the proof plates by hand. Some of the plates, like Plate 89, were engraved for him by John G. Warnicke, who died in 1818, and others by Alexander Lawson.

An able naturalist, he wrote better descriptions than the more famous J. J. Audubon (see below). Wilson was helped in the acquisition of specimens by Meriwether Lewis, an explorer, who had been out west as far as the Pacific and who brought back several new species of bird which he gave to Wilson to illustrate. When he could not otherwise obtain a specimen to copy, he had to find and shoot one, sometimes travelling great distances to do so. Thus he had to be explorer, hunter and marksman as well as author and artist. As the work advanced, he had help from local artists, under the supervision of Alexander Rider, in the colouring of the engravings from his samples. Wilson's legacy to America was more than his famous book. He inspired artists to use the wilderness and its flourishing wildlife as their subject-matter, and writers and poets to describe the wild America he loved.

Great though the achievements of Wilson were, they were soon outshone by those of JOHN JAMES LAFOREST AUDUBON (1785–1851), a colourful extrovert. He was born in Santo Domingo, now the Dominican Republic, the illegitimate son of a French naval officer and a creole French woman who died only seven months after the boy was born. When he was five years old, his father returned to his home, near Nantes in France, where Mrs Audubon, to her credit, accepted young John into the family as if he were her own son. The lad had minimal schooling. His interest lay in the countryside where he could draw birds and observe the world of nature.

In 1805 his father sent him to manage Mill Grove, the estate that he had bought near Philadelphia, and to develop the lead mines on the land. But his heart was not in the task. He preferred to be out walking in the woods to writing office ledgers. He was such an inept manager that he lost his house and job. Undaunted, he and a friend set off on a thousand-mile trek to Louisville, where they established a shop selling 'dry goods'. While his more businesslike and ambitious friend ran the store, Audubon went out to study and collect birds. In Louisville, Audubon met Alexander Wilson who was on a collecting expedition. Wilson's paintings for his proposed book may well have given Audubon the idea for his own.

Things did not go well, so Audubon and his partner moved downriver to Henderson, Kentucky, to start a new venture there. In 1808 Audubon married a girl he had met near Philadelphia. Even with her encouragement, the new enterprise, and some other business ventures to which he later turned, all collapsed. His two daughters died and, having wasted much of his wife's inheritance, he found himself in the debtors' prison, deprived of freedom and friends. These were hard times indeed.

On his release he continued to add to his collection of life-sized paintings of birds. In order to make his subjects more natural, he devised a system of wiring the bird specimens into credible postures. However, looking at many of the pictures, it is clear that he was not always successful, many of the birds being in positions more likely to be found when dead (Plate 90). He had to contort some of the larger birds (their necks, for example) in order to fit the birds onto one page. He often corrected his paintings. If this could not be achieved otherwise, he glued a piece of paper painted with the new version over the error. It is a fascinating exercise to examine the original watercolours at the New York Historical Society, to see where, and how skilfully, he has done this.

In 1820 Audubon set out to sail down the Mississippi river with his thirteen-year-old student, Joseph Mason, who was already a gifted painter of landscapes and contributed more than fifty of the backgrounds in Audubon's paintings. Audubon's hopes of publishing his proposed major work, *The Birds of America*, met with no support in America chiefly because of the size and quality of the engravings required and the magnitude of the publishing task.

Audubon sailed from New Orleans to Liverpool in 1826 where he was welcomed and his paintings were acclaimed. He soon arranged with William Lizars, of Edinburgh, to make and print the first group of engravings of some colourful and significant birds. But there were labour problems with the colourers so that the work could not proceed in Scotland. In London, Audubon secured the help of Robert Havell (Jr) who saw the work right through to completion of the 435 huge, 100×75cm (39½×29½in), plates. Keeping funds coming in to pay for the continuing production and the hand colouring of the aquatints, and finding more species to illustrate, meant that

1. *Passenger Pigeon.* 2. *Blue-mountain Warbler.* 3. *Hemlock W.*

89   *Passenger Pigeon, Blue-mountain Warbler and Hemlock Warbler*
After ALEXANDER WILSON (1766–1813)
Hand-coloured copper engraving by John G. Warnicke (?–1818), 26.7×34 cm (10½×13½ in)

Wilson has shown three different birds in the one plate to save space and printing costs. The passenger pigeon used to be very common in North America, occurring in huge flocks, but it was hunted to extinction

90   *Red-headed Woodpeckers*
After JOHN JAMES LAFOREST AUDUBON (1785–1851)
Hand-coloured aquatint, 98×63 cm (38½×23¾ in) by Robert Havell (Jr)

Male and female adult and immature birds are shown around a dead tree-trunk where they nest and the beetle grubs on which they feed occur. A serious, if unconvincing, attempt has been made to make the scene look lifelike

Drawn from Nature & Published by John J. Audubon F.R.S.E. M.W.S.

Engraved, Printed & Coloured by R.Havell & Son, London.

Red headed Woodpecker. Male 1 F 2 Young 3. 4. 5.
PICUS ERYTHROCEPHALUS.

PLATE LXVI.

SCAUP POCHARD, FEM.

Audubon had to cross the Atlantic several times. Like Wilson, he had to hunt and shoot the specimens that he needed, sometimes killing more than a hundred birds in a day. It has been said that after he had skinned the birds, he ate them.

A young Scottish naturalist, William MacGillivray, assisted Audubon in writing the text. Audubon's project was finally finished in 1838, thirty years after it had begun, amid acclamation from both sides of the Atlantic for the success of a remarkable achievement, as much in sheer perseverance in the face of enormous obstacles as in the quality of the work. On his return to America at the age of fifty-seven, he announced his proposal to publish a new work, *The Quadrupeds of North America* (see below) and a smaller, 28×20cm (11×8in) edition of *The Birds of America*.

From America we turn now to consider a British painter of birds only a few years younger than Audubon. PRIDEAUX JOHN SELBY (1788–1867) had a privileged upbringing in the North of England. As a boy he had a particular interest in birds and kept careful sketches of, and notes about, them. He made a collection of skins of birds he himself had shot. Like other young country gentlemen, he was adept both with his gun and fishing rod.

Soon after he had finished his education at the University of Oxford, he inherited from his father a large country estate in the county of Northumberland. In addition to managing his lands, he contributed, as country squires were expected to do then, to the life of the community by being a magistrate and high sheriff of the county. With his income secure, he was able to give his support to natural history and other learned societies. He was elected a Fellow of the Linnean Society of London and of the Royal Society of Edinburgh. Selby, who was in the process of publishing his book by then, met J. J. Audubon while he was in Edinburgh in 1826 and, with the Dumfries artist-naturalist Sir

William Jardine (who was co-author with Selby of *Illustrations of Ornithology* (1826–43)), had some lessons in painting from Audubon.

Plate 91 shows a picture from Selby's *Illustrations of British Ornithology, or Figures of British Birds Their Full Natural Size* (1821–34). This was his major work, based on his drawings of birds in his collection of mounted skins. He etched the plates himself and then took them to William Lizars in Edinburgh to be touched up and printed. Published in parts without any associated text, it was a collection of 69×54cm (27×21in) copper-plate etchings of birds, all but the very largest rendered life size. The nineteen parts, in hand-coloured and uncoloured versions, were published over thirteen years on a variety of papers and were usually bound into two volumes, land birds (89 plates) and water birds (129 plates). Most of the colouring of the etchings was carefully and accurately done by a young artist, Daniel McNee, who was working for Lizars at the time and who later became a successful portrait painter in Glasgow. However, as Plate 91 shows, the colouring of some plates was less than exact.

Selby's *Illustrations* was so popular that there were several printings. He later produced a small number of copies of a descriptive text which, on the advice of Lizars, he kept separate from the plates. In 1842 he published *A Brief History of British Forest Trees*, with detailed text describing all native British species, the illustrations being wood engravings of his drawings, largely of the numerous varieties growing on his own and neighbouring estates.

Although etching has had a long history despite being unfashionable between the 1940s and the 1970s, it is now being used again very effectively. PETER PARTINGTON (see page 65) has, in recent years, been in the forefront among wildlife artists to turn again to etching which had, with engravings, lost popularity in England by the outbreak of World War II. As Plate 92 shows, Peter uses a delightfully free style in the etching and then colours each print afterwards with watercolours. From the artist's and buyer's point of view, this technique has much to commend it. One good idea for a picture (the most precious single asset any good artist can have) can be made into a series of prints, each personally made by the artist, which can be sold at a price that many more people can

afford than if the same idea had been made into one painting only.

Having considered the artists who depicted birds in etchings and engravings, we next look at those who, using similar techniques, specialised in animals and fish.

Marcus Elieser Bloch (1723–99), of whom little is known, left one claim to fame: he published, in Berlin, what has been called the most beautiful book on fish ever produced, *Ichthyologie, ou Histoire Naturelle Générale et Particulière des Poissons* (1785–97). The copper engravings were made by various experts, of whom Ludewig Schmidt (active 1780s) was probably the best. Plates 93 and 94 were engraved by him, Plate 94 being from a painting by 'Kruger jun.', of whom nothing is known.

Where Bloch's book was the leader in fish, the key book on American mammals contained fine prints depicting both the animal and its habitat and was by JOHN WOODHOUSE AUDUBON (1812–62), the younger son of John James who taught him the 'Audubon method' of painting. He contributed nearly half the paintings of animals (Plate 95) for his father's *The Viviparous Quadrupeds of North America* (1845–8), originally published in folio size (52×34cm [20½×13½]). For the text Audubon was assisted by his sons John Woodhouse and Victor Gifford, and by his friend the Rev John Bachman, who described their aim in the foreword:

We have endeavoured to place before the public a series of plates which are not only scientifically correct, but interesting to all, from the varied occupations, expressions, and attitudes we have given to the different species, together with the appropriate accessories such as trees, plants and landscapes, etc, with which the animals are relieved.

The importance that they placed upon demonstrating the natural habitat of the animals was thus emphasised, a view very much in line with scientific thought today. The elder Audubon son, Victor Gifford, helped the publication by painting some of the backgrounds and by managing the technical aspects of finance and publication.

HERBERT THOMAS DICKSEE (1862–1942) was the son of Thomas Francis Dicksee, the painter of

92 *Two Hares*
PETER PARTINGTON (1941–)
Hand-coloured etching, 20×29 cm (8×11½ in)

The alertness and serenity of hares in a flower
meadow are cleverly captured in this simple,
evocative composition. The colours are restrained,
the detail minimal, yet there are sufficient of both
and more of either would not have improved the
picture. This is what art is all about

(Opposite above)
93 *The Blue Fish*
After an unknown artist
Hand-coloured engraving in blue ink, Ludewig
Schmidt (active 1780s) 19×37.5 cm (7½×14¾ in)

While unashamedly primarily an illustration, the
superb drawing and colouring still makes this a good
picture. In order to indicate the thickness of the fish
a transverse section through the abdomen is shown
below the tail

(Opposite below)
94 *The Orf*
After 'KRUGER JUN.' (dates unknown)
Hand-coloured engraving in orange ink by Ludewig
Schmidt (active 1780s), 19×37.5 cm (7½×14¾ in)

Exquisite colouring here includes silver-looking
paint on the scales. The clean, fresh colours are
largely due to the fact that the basic print was made
in such a carefully selected blue ink. Black would
have ruined this

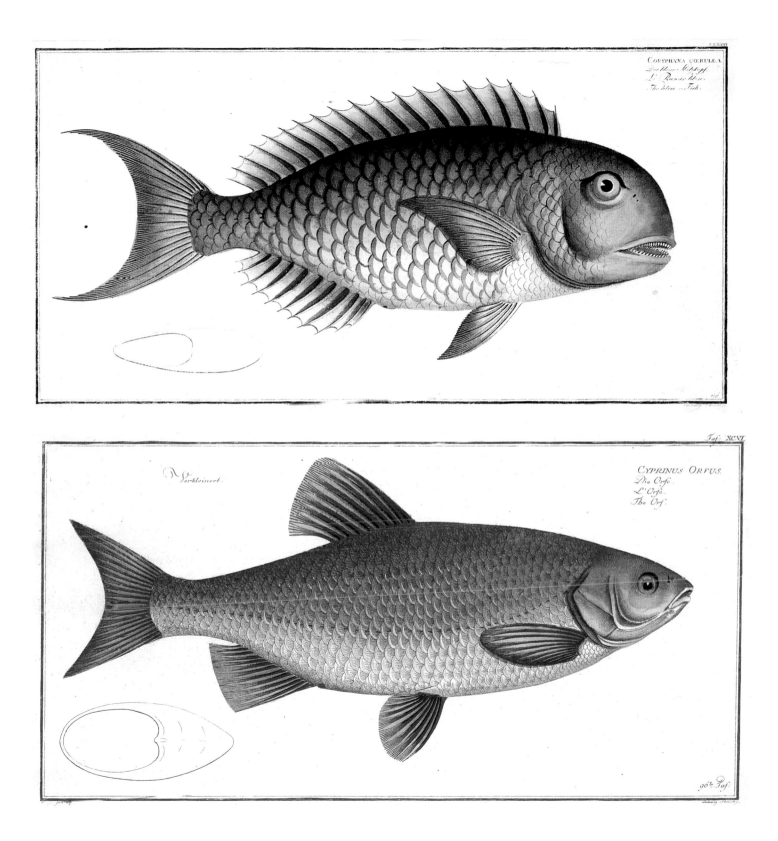

CORYPHÆNA COERULEA.
Der blaue Stichkopf.
L. Rascasseur.
The blue Fish.

Verkleinert.

CYPRINUS ORFUS.
Die Orfe.
L'Orfe.
The Orf.

95 *Mexican Marmot-Squirrel (male)*
After JOHN WOODHOUSE AUDUBON (1812–62)
Lithographed, printed and coloured by J. T. Bowen,
46×57 cm (18×22½ in)

Apart from the life-size portrait of the ground
squirrel, here is a lovely lithographic landscape.
Habitat and creature are given equal importance

portraits and historical genre scenes. His brother,
Sir Frank Dicksee, and his sister, Miss Margaret
Isabel Dicksee, were also painters. Herbert,
having studied at the Slade School of Art, was a
painter and etcher of animal scenes, particularly of
lions (Plate 96) and taught drawing at the City of
London School. He exhibited at the Royal Academy 1885–1904 and was elected a Fellow of the
Royal Society of Painter-Etchers and Engravers in

1885. Plate 96 is an etching made by Herbert the
year after his original painting was exhibited in
the Royal Academy in 1897. Current reference
books say little about Herbert, who was outshone
by his more famous brother Frank. This may have
been at least partly because Herbert specialised in
animals, which were less fashionable in art circles
than Frank's genre scenes.

Here we turn from etchings and engravings of animals to those of flowers.

Dr Robert John Thornton (*c*1765–1837),
described on an engraved portrait of him as 'Public Lecturer on Medical Botany' (at Guy's Hospital, London), lived at a time when, particularly in
Europe, there was a great surge of interest in
flowers and some beautifully illustrated botanical

books were published. He decided to show that
the British could do even better and aimed to produce the most magnificent botanical book ever
published, 57×46cm (22½×18in). His plan was to
print a three-part work, two of text and one of
plates printed in colour and then hand coloured.
This third part he called *Temple of Flora or Garden of
Nature* and published it one plate at a time from
1797 to 1807. The plates for the first edition,
51×38cm (20×15in), were produced unsystematically but, since each is dated, it has been possible
to show the order in which they were issued. The
reproduction methods were a mixture of aquatint,
stipple (another etching technique) and engraving.

Thornton engaged a group of competent artists
to prepare the illustrations, the first of whom
(1790) was PHILIP REINAGLE (1749–1833). He had

established a reputation for paintings of sporting scenes and some landscapes and portraits. He was elected an Associate of the Royal Academy in 1788 and Academician in 1812. Thornton arranged for Reinagle to paint the flower for his fourth plate but engaged Abraham Pether (1756–1812), noted for his moonlight landscapes which earned him the nickname 'Moonlight Pether', to paint the background. A second edition was published in 1812 with a smaller, 25×18cm (10×7in), format and, in some cases, different artists (Plate 97). It is not known why Reinagle was asked to paint a new version of the *Strelitzia* (called the Queen Flower

after Charlotte, wife of George III) for the second edition, but the work is undoubtedly better than that by Peter Henderson for the first edition.

At this point we make a major change and consider a completely different technique for printing an image – lithography. This was invented in Germany in 1798 and was at its best in the nineteenth century. A mirror image of the intended picture was drawn on a flat slab of porous, fine-grained stone using greasy crayons. Next the stone was wetted with water and then covered with an oily ink which adhered only to the parts of the stone

which had been greased in the drawing. Damp paper was then applied to the stone and printed with a special press. The prints were then coloured by hand. Lithographs have a 'soft' character, as

96 *Raiders*
HERBERT THOMAS DICKSEE (1862–1942)
Hand-coloured etching dated 1898, 41×66 cm (16×26 in)

This etching is a copy by Dicksee of the painting by him which was exhibited in the Royal Academy in 1897. It shows something of the sense of drama that was popular in paintings then

though drawn with pencil, and are completely different from the sharp black lines of engravings.

The greatest exponent of lithography in natural history books was JOHN GOULD (1804–81), an industrious and remarkably successful artist, publisher and systematic ornithologist. Born in Lyme Regis, Dorset, he spent his boyhood in the countryside near Guildford, Surrey. His special interest in birds began very early when his father showed him the nest of a hedge sparrow and its blue eggs. He had little formal schooling and no university education. As an artist he was self-taught. As a naturalist he was more single-minded than most of his contemporaries. While many of them were simultaneously interested in numerous aspects of natural history and contemporary discoveries but expert in none, he unashamedly confined his interest to birds (with the one exception of Australian mammals).

From an early age Gould's business acumen was evident. While apprenticed as a gardener at Windsor at the age of fourteen, he learned many of the skills of the taxidermist and sold blown birds' eggs to boys at Eton College. When he was only twenty, Gould established a taxidermy business in London. Three years later he was appointed 'Curator and Preserver to the Museum' of the newly established Zoological Society of London. He was commissioned by King George IV to stuff various birds and animals, including his giraffe. All this experience, together with the opportunity to meet at the Zoological Society the leading biologists of the time, provided him with an invaluable background to his future career.

In 1829 Gould married Elizabeth Coxon, whose two brothers had emigrated to Australia. The skills of man and wife were ideally complementary. Having acquired a collection of skins of Himalayan birds, mostly new to British naturalists, Gould stuffed them and saw their potential as the basis for his first book, containing eighty plates depicting a hundred birds, *A Century of Birds*

97 *The Queen Flower*
PHILIP REINAGLE (1749–1833)
Hand-coloured aquatint, 24.5×18.5 cm (9½×7¼ in)

More than just a flower portrait, this shows also the habitat. The view of the distant river, the palms and hills make this at once both an accurate illustration and a pleasing picture

Hitherto Unfigured from the Himalaya Mountains (1830–3). Gould made the drawings and his wife copied them onto the lithographic stones.

The next Gould book was much more ambitious, *The Birds of Europe* (1832–7). While Elizabeth Gould contributed many of the plates for this, sixty-eight were made by Edward Lear (see over). Lear was aggrieved to find that for some of the plates, even though his signature appeared in the lithograph, the caption read 'Drawn from nature and on stone by J. & E. Gould'. In other instances Gould used Lear's work without any acknowledgement whatever. Because there are many plates in Gould's early publications that have no signature and no attribution, it may never be possible to know for certain whether they are the work of Gould and his wife or of Lear. Even if Gould's early attributions cast some doubt on his

98 *Montagu's Harrier*
After JOHN GOULD (1804–81)
Hand-coloured lithograph by H. C. Richter, 36×53 cm (14×21 in)

The grey of the male gave rise to its old scientific name *cineraceus*, meaning ashy. Now called *Circus pygargus*, it is seen here eating a dead mole. Note the characteristic 'softness' in the lithographic image

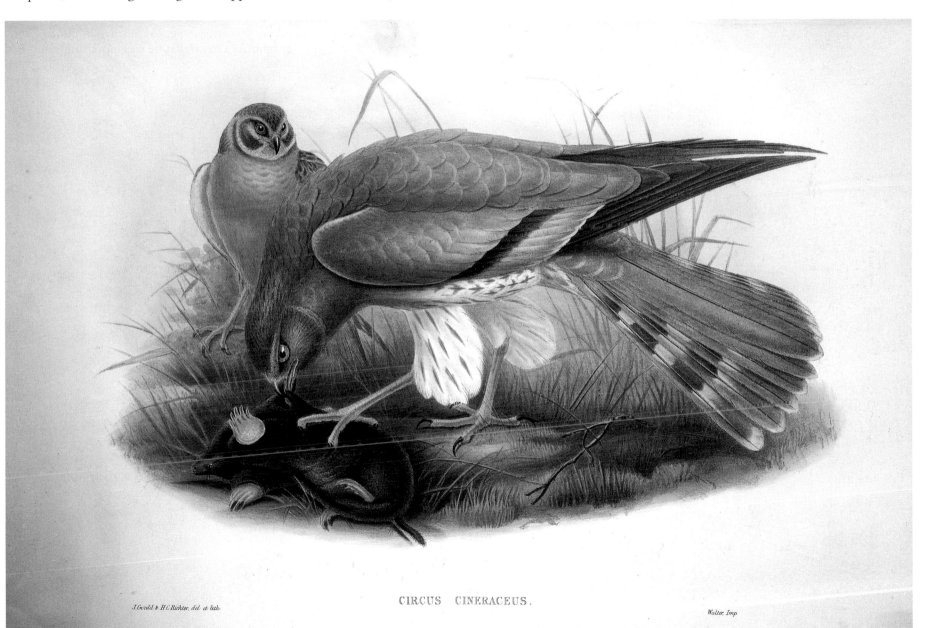

J. Gould & H. C. Richter, del. et lith.

CIRCUS CINERACEUS.

Walter, Imp.

integrity, what followed showed him to be a great man, willing to give honour where honour was due, particularly with regard to his naming of the first person to describe a species. So much was achieved, it could only have been done because he was an adept organiser, persuading others to work in his team with enthusiasm and skill. Twenty-eight other major works followed, superbly illustrated with lithographs. Among these were monographs on toucans (1833–5), the birds of Australia (1840–8), the partridges of America (1844–50) and the birds of Great Britain (1862–73) (see Plate 98).

For most people today EDWARD LEAR (1812–88) is best known for his Nonsense poems, a fact that would greatly disappoint this man of many gifts, since these were written only for light-hearted amusement while he laboured on what he saw as his real work. Born the twentieth of twenty-one children, he was largely brought up by his elder sister Ann. He was a sickly child and prone all his life to attacks of depression and epilepsy. Encouraged to draw by his sister, he had to earn his own living as a draughtsman from the age of sixteen. At first he drew diseased organs for doctors of medicine and coloured screens, fans and prints. But he soon specialised in drawing birds and studied the parrots at the Zoological Society of London following an introduction by a Mrs Wentworth. At the early age of nineteen, in spite of his rudimentary education and poor eyesight, he published his first book, *Illustrations of The Family of Psittacidae, Or Parrots . . .* (1832). This contained forty-two life-size lithographs of his superb drawings (Plate 99). Having satisfied himself that he had accurately rendered the posture, plumage and colours, he personally traced the drawings onto the lithographic stones. When the prints from the stones were made, he checked each carefully for its blackness and sharpness. The prints were then hand coloured by others under his supervision. For one of his age to achieve all this is a remarkable testimony to his skill and maturity.

The precision of his drawing and the accuracy and beauty of his colouring established new criteria for book illustrations of birds. He contributed sixty-eight lithographs to *The Birds of Europe* by John Gould (see page 133). In 1831 Lord Stanley, son of the Earl of Derby, appointed Lear to make drawings of the birds and animals in his menagerie at Knowsley Hall. It was while he was there that he wrote and illustrated, for the entertainment of the children of the family, his humorous verse and limericks, first published in *A Book of Nonsense* (1846).

His aim was to become a landscape painter rather than an ornithological illustrator, so in 1837 he gave up his natural history pursuits in London and at Knowsley Hall. He went to Rome where he lived for most of the next ten years and published a book of illustrations of Rome and its environs, followed later by a book of illustrated excursions in Italy. From 1848 onwards he made numerous tours of Malta, Greece and its Aegean islands, Turkey and the Middle East including Egypt. From the mid-1850s, he spent an increasing amount of time abroad, mostly in Italy, until he died in San Remo, Italy.

Lear's career was a sad one. Society then was even less sympathetic to an epileptic than it is now. For many years he submitted work to the Royal Academy and as often had it rejected. His paintings were appreciated by a discerning few but spurned by the majority. Queen Victoria was so impressed by Lear's book about travel in Italy that she asked him to give her drawing lessons. But later (1850), still very conscious of the fact that he was self-taught, he humbly enrolled as a probationer student at the Academy. It was in the same year that he first had work accepted there.

His long absences abroad prevented him from building up an expanding market for his paintings. He tended to overprice them and consequently they did not sell. He was always short of money and (unwisely) decided to mass-produce a large number of deliberately cheap watercolours to attract more customers. While he succeeded in this, the deteriorating quality of his paintings and his lack of discernment in assessing his own work led to an erosion of confidence in those of his patrons who had bought his more expensive pieces. But through all these difficulties there shines the constant light of his irrepressible humour. It was in the year of his death that the first printing of his collected four *Nonsense* books was published.

From the surface prints of lithographs we turn to consider relief prints made from blocks of wood and linoleum. Wood engravings are made by cutting into the end grain of seasoned blocks of hardwood such as box or yew after the surface has been made absolutely flat and smooth. After completion of the engraving, the surface of the block is coated with ink with a roller, taking care that the ink does not get down into the incised grooves. Wood-block printing is, therefore, the opposite of metal engraving. Paper is then pressed onto the block (or vice versa) so that the unengraved parts transmit the ink to the paper but the incised parts leave clean white areas.

Woodcuts are different from wood engravings. Incisions are made along the line of the grain of a slab of wood, usually of softwoods. The technique was invented in China about the ninth century AD and has its modern counterpart in linocuts. In both wood engravings and woodcuts, the grain of the wood may be deliberately used by the artist to impart a pattern to the design. Blocks using the cross grain of hardwood had the great advantage that they could be used in a mechanical printing press for much longer than ones relying on the long grain of softer woods. Lino, of course, has no grain in the smooth surface of the sheet. Otherwise its use is virtually the same as for woodcuts.

The term 'wood-block print' is a less precise term, simply indicating the material of the printing block and the method of image transfer as compared with metal engravings, for example. It is applied equally to wood engravings and woodcuts, although it usually refers to the latter in oriental prints.

Anyone investigating the subject of wood engraving for the first time will soon come upon the name of THOMAS BEWICK (1753–1828). He and his work were famous in his lifetime and have inspired a stream of books and articles about him since. More than one hundred and fifty years after his death his brilliantly skilful wood engravings are still being used as illustrations. His early talent at drawing was helped when at the age of fourteen

99 *Blue and Yellow Mackaw*
EDWARD LEAR (1812–88)
Hand-coloured lithograph, 53.5×35.5 cm (21×14 in)

Here is amazingly mature draughtsmanship and colouring for an artist aged no more than nineteen. The manuscript note at the foot of the print was added in the last century

MACROCERCUS ARARAUNA.

Blue & Yellow Maccaw.

⅞ Nat Size.

Lear, Illustrations of the family of Psittacidæ. 1832.

100 *The Great Auk*
THOMAS BEWICK (1753–1828)
Wood engraving, 8.3×8.1 cm (3¼×3 in actual image),
enlarged to show detail in the wood block carving

This is one of the engravings from Bewick's *British
Birds*. The illustrations were printed on both sides of
the book page. Since the paper was thin, original
engravings usually show evidence of the printing on
the other side

101 *The Corvorant*
THOMAS BEWICK (1753–1828)
Wood engraving, 8.6×7.5 cm (3¼×3 in)

Not only does Bewick accurately indicate the
features of this fish-eating seabird (now called a
cormorant), but he manages to squeeze into the
picture a sailing boat. Each white spot or line is made
by carving away the wood

he was apprenticed to an engraver (mostly of metal) in Newcastle. By the conclusion of his apprenticeship he had learned a wide variety of skills and made many important contacts with people of wealth and influence. After a short time working in London, which did not appeal to him, he returned to Newcastle and later established a partnership with his former teacher, Ralph Beilby.

Bewick's two greatest works, *A General History of the Quadrupeds* (1790) and *A History of British Birds* (1797–1804), were published during this partnership. Beilby wrote the text, largely copied from books of the day, for the volume on the *Quadrupeds* and for the first of the two volumes of *British Birds*, while Bewick provided the numerous wood engravings for the illustrations (Plates 100, 101) and the tailpieces to chapters etc. When Bewick discovered that Beilby was intending to put only his own name as the author of the first volume of *Birds*, a dispute ensued and was settled only by a committee of their friends. It was agreed that the first volume should have no author's name but only 'Printed for Beilby and Bewick by Edward Walker of Newcastle'. Bewick then bought Beilby's share of the rights for the remaining copies of the two volumes of *Birds* and for the *Quadrupeds* for £400. This meant that Bewick had to provide the text as well as the illustrations for the second volume of *Birds*, which necessarily slowed the publication.

Bewick was born in a farmhouse in Cherryburn on the south bank of the River Tyne about ten miles west of Newcastle-upon-Tyne, now preserved as a museum by the National Trust. In 1827 John James Audubon, the American illustrator and writer, called on Bewick and had tea with him. He described him as 'a perfect old Englishman, full of life, although seventy-four years of age, active and prompt in his labours . . . a son of Nature to which he owed nearly all that characterised him as an artist and a man . . .'

The influence of Bewick on book illustration continues, like the popularity of his wood engravings. His technique also survives the pressures from its contemporary competitors, whereas engraving on metal plates virtually ceased more than a hundred years ago. Although, naturally, a host of other styles have been used, some engravers in wood still try to emulate the delicacy of Bewick's carving and subtlety of design.

A living British artist using much the same wood-engraving techniques as Bewick, producing monochrome prints of natural history subjects, is COLIN PAYNTON. Born in 1946 in Bedfordshire, he trained at the Northampton School of Art. He first worked as a painter in London but moved to Wales in 1972, where he still lives in a remote farmhouse. A self-taught wood engraver, his interest in wood-block printing developed some five years later. After only five more years he had his engravings first exhibited at the Royal Society of Painter-Etchers and Engravers and he was elected a Fellow in 1986. In addition to being in the permanent collection at NATURE IN ART, his work is included in the Ashmolean Museum, Oxford, and the National Library of Wales, and the Berlin Graphothek. His engravings have illustrated eleven books.

Colin was attracted to wood engraving by the purity of the clean-edged, contrasting black and white in the prints (Plates 102, 103). He writes:

Making a wood engraving is by its nature a very unforgiving process (the opportunity to rework a block is limited indeed) and this too I find irresistible and challenging. Much of the subject-matter of my work stems from my long-standing interest in natural history, particularly ornithology. Following this theme, I hoped to continue something of a tradition among wood engravers, past and present – a tradition having its roots in Thomas Bewick's well-known books of birds and quadrupeds. From time to time, commissioned work provides an added challenge, taking me away from the familiar territory of wildlife subjects.

As practised by wood engravers such as Bewick and Paynton, their engravings produce images of one colour (usually black) contrasting with the un-inked paper. Not only was monochrome wood-block printing first developed in China but it was also there that multicoloured wood-block printing first began.

Nature had been a favourite theme for wood-block artists in China since the early seventeenth century when the expert engraver HOU YUE-TS'ONG first published them in *The Ten Bamboo Studio Albums* (1619–33). Like many others published then and since, such oriental illustrated books had the double purpose of being a picture book for the collector and a copy-book for trainee artists. The title came from the ten bamboos growing outside the house where the small group of artists met in Nanking. The book contained superb multicoloured wood-block prints (Plate 104), made from paintings by the group, and also included monochromatic prints in black and orange, together with instructions for artists on how to paint bamboos and a print showing how to hold the brush correctly (Plate 105). Throughout the sixteen slim volumes originally published, bamboos form an important part of the subject-matter (Plate 106).

The technique of multicoloured wood-block printing which the Chinese had begun was taken to new heights of craftsmanship and sophistication by the Japanese. They appear to have discovered, in the seventeenth century, the feasibility of making prints of several different colours all incorporated in the one picture. By the nineteenth century they had become great experts in producing superb multicoloured wood-block prints. For these the Japanese made woodcuts, using the long grain of the wood, rather than the cross grain favoured by the English wood engravers like Bewick.

In the seventeenth century the Japanese became fascinated by paintings of genre scenes, depicting people in all manner of activities. They called these 'fleeting, floating world pictures': *ukiyo-e*, a term applied in the first instance to paintings. The coloured wood-block print technique was rapidly assimilated by the 'floating world' painters, so much so that virtually all the coloured wood-block prints then were of such scenes and so *all* wood block prints have sometimes been lumped together in the term *ukiyo-e*. Strictly speaking, the term *ukiyo-e* should be used only to describe the subject-matter – genre scenes – and not the coloured wood-block print technique in general or prints depicting wildlife subjects (which form a very small proportion) in particular.

Even though richly coloured natural history subjects such as trees, flowers and animals appeared in Japanese paintings and screens in the late sixteenth century, wildlife was not the subject of wood-block prints until the early part of the nineteenth century. Japanese publishers of prints employed expert artists to make the designs,

102 *Mute Swan and Carp*
COLIN PAYNTON (1946–)
Wood engraving, 22.5×27.5 cm (9×10¾ in)

Preliminary pencil sketches:
(a) First trial layout (above left)
(b) Swans and carp redrawn (left)
(c, d) Swallows (above)
(e) Final engraving (opposite). Typical of his work, this shows what is happening simultaneously above and below the water. Swirling ripples in the water surface unite the design

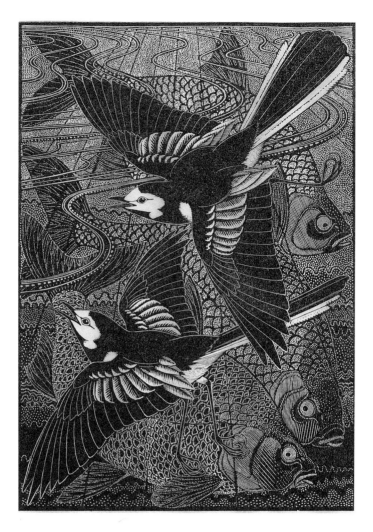

103 *Pied Wagtail and Roach*
COLIN PAYNTON (1946–)
Wood engraving, 13×9 cm (5×3½ in)

These attractive, agile birds catch insects by flying
swiftly after them. Their quick movements contrast
with the lazy great fish below the surface of the lake

(Opposite)
104 *White Bird and Snow on a Branch of Camellia*
TEN BAMBOO STUDIO ARTIST (1619–33)
Wood-block print in five colours, 24×26 cm
(9¼×10¼ in)

With each colour applied by a different wood block,
this is a splendid example of early use of this
technique. The whiteness of the snow and the bird is
shown by applying grey ink around them. This
photograph is of a copy in its original book. The
central part of the picture, made by two separate
blocks (one for each page), is partly obscured in the
binding

105 *Instructions on How to Paint*
TEN BAMBOO STUDIO ARTIST (1619–33), 1719 reprint
Wood-block print in black, 24×26 cm (9¼×10¼ in)

A relaxed, free-hand method of holding the brush is
shown. The long finger nails suggest that artists then
were not expected to do manual labour

起手執筆式

海陽胡正言同淡甫輯選
高陽秋甫氏校正
淩雲翰五雲甫
吳士冠相如甫
魏之璜考叔甫
魏之克和叔甫
胡宗智佰通甫
高友三盖甫
釋行一靜涵甫仝校

140

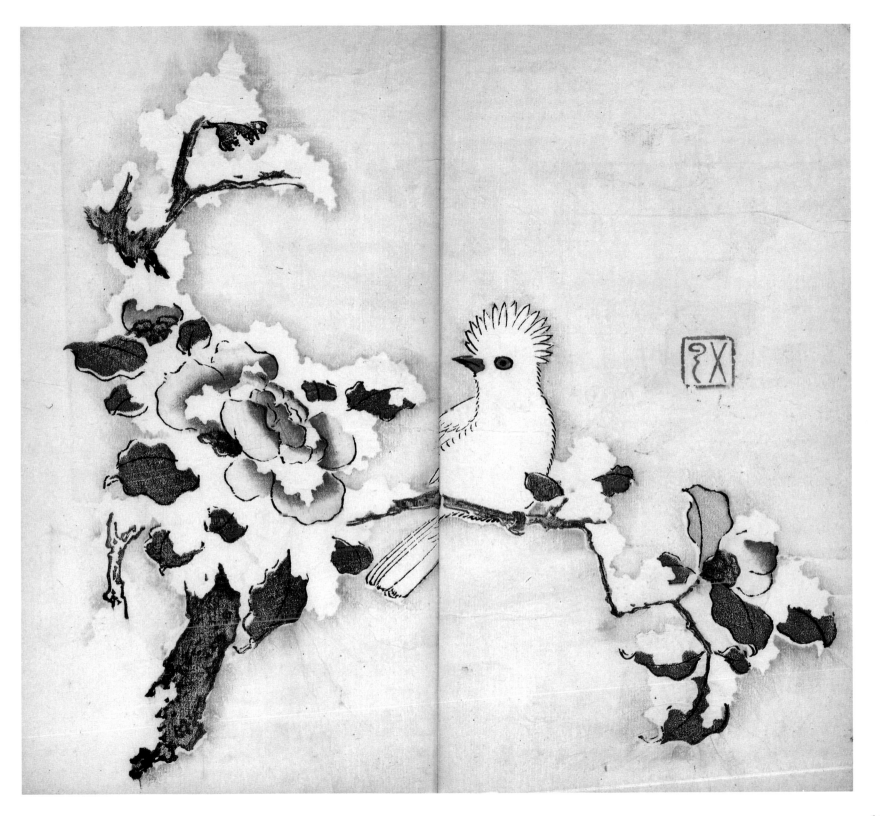

cutters to create the blocks and printers to print them, much as many artists in Europe had the help of metal engravers and printers in making their prints. So far as images of nature are concerned, the use of this technique reached its peak in the early part of the twentieth century.

In addition to the different colours printed by each of the individual blocks, embossing of the paper was also produced by suitably carved blocks, a feature which was sometimes added to the colour printing to lend texture to the subject and to create a more three-dimensional effect (Plate 107b).

Before looking at the twentieth-century Japanese artists using a multiple wood-block technique, we must briefly consider the print artist from Edo, NAKAYAMA SUGAKUDO (active 1860s and 1870s), who is the earliest multiple-colour wood-block artist represented in the permanent collection at NATURE IN ART. Plate 107 is the thirty-eighth from a series of wood-block prints designed by Sugakudo entitled *Forty-eight Sketches of Birds and Flowers*, each of which is framed in a bright yellow border. Louise Norton Brown (1924) described it as 'one of the most charming works of its kind in existence'. Sugakudo designed a second part to this collection in 1858 and a second set of prints in 1861 depicting birds and flowers of the four seasons.

106 *Bamboo*
TEN BAMBOO STUDIO ARTIST (1619–33), 1719 reprint.
Wood-block print in black, 24×26 cm (9¼×10¼ in)

The charm of this print, and its very essence, is utter simplicity

107 *Shrike, Camellia and Oak*
NAKAYAMA SUGAKUDO (active 1860s and 1870s)
Wood-block print in five colours and embossed,
36×24.5 cm (14×9½ in), dated '11th month 1859'

(a) The tablets top right describe the title of the print and the series, the writing lower right is the signature of the artist (above his seal) and the seals in the yellow left margin indicate (*top*) the month and year of publication, (*centre*) the plate number (38), and (*bottom*) the publisher
(b) Detail by tangential lighting showing the embossing of the paper of the bird and background but sparing the leaves etc

SHOSON (1877–1945) specialised in woodblock prints of wildlife (Plates 108, 109). Strongly influenced by traditional ways of rendering certain subjects established by Hokusai (1760–1849), Hiroshige (1797–1858) and others, he developed his own style with great originality. By the time he produced Plates 108 and 109, he had broken free of the stylised rendering of birds which had been fashionable and, with charming restraint in his choice of colours and great facility in composition, he created a new realism. In 1912 he changed his print publisher from Taihei and moved to Watanabe, who now began adding their small circular seal to the prints. At the same time, as artists frequently did, he changed his name to Koson and thus his signature and seal (Plate 110). Hokusai used at least thirty different working names at various times (and sometimes different names at the same time) in his distinguished career of fifty working years!

108 *Waxwings*
SHOSON (1877–1945)
Wood-block print in five colours, 33.5×18.5 cm
(13×7 in)

The colours varying as subtly as in a painting, this charming composition could be confused with one. The pattern of the long grain of the wood apparent in the gently coloured background shows that it is a wood-block print

109 *Eagle in the Snow*
SHOSON (1877–1945)
Wood-block print in four colours, 42×25.5 cm
(16½×10 in)

Superbly restrained use of colour and clever composition make this a triumph. How feeble it would be if the bird was looking the other way or if the twigs coming in from the top were not there! Note the tiny blue streaks on the bird's back

110 *Carp*
KOSON (1877–1945)
Wood-block print in five colours, 36.5×23.5 cm
(14¼×9¼ in)

Another masterpiece of simple composition by the same artist as Plates 108 and 109 but under the new name he assumed in 1912. Movement is indicated by the streaks in the water made by deliberately uneven inking of the block at each 'pull'. Each print is thus slightly different

Traders, missionaries and diplomats who visited Japan in the nineteenth century brought back these wood-block prints to Europe. There collectors were interested in prints and oriental objects before Western artists more slowly came to appreciate the sensitivity and charm of this technique. Although printing in colours from wood-blocks had been known in Europe for three hundred years, it was not until the end of the nineteenth century that European artists began to try their hand at, and adapt, this direct technique of making colour prints. Before this time, the practice had been to make prints in one colour (usually, but not always black) from engravings in metal or wood, or lithographs, etc which were then coloured by hand.

Among those inspired by imported Japanese multicoloured wood-block prints in the second half of the nineteenth century was Professor ALLEN WILLIAM SEABY (see page 19 and Plate 112). Unlike most Japanese print designers, he cut his own wood-blocks. Robert Gillmor (see page 150) has kindly lent NATURE IN ART a short typed description by Seaby, *Colour Printing from Wood Blocks*, which he wrote about 1925:

About thirty years ago Mr F. Morley Fletcher was teaching art in Reading, and formed a class for producing colour prints from wood blocks. Since then, through his teaching, or indirectly through his book on the subject, many art workers in Britain and America have interested themselves in the process, and it may fairly be

111 *Cherry Blossom*
SHIN SUI ITO (1896–)
Wood-block print in seven colours, 40.5×27 cm (16×10½ in)

The delicacy with which these blocks must have been carved is well shown here by the thin lines surrounding petals and leaves. The registration of the individual colours is precise

112 *Bullfinches*
ALLEN WILLIAM SEABY (1867–1953)
Wood-block print in four colours, 21.5×21.5 cm (8½×8½ in)

While this shows clear Japanese influence, it also indicates the individuality of the artist. There have been two separate applications of a blue: compare the snow and the rump of the birds

147

said that Block Printing in Colour is one of the most important of the practical art movements of recent times, although almost unrecognised by official bodies such as the Royal Academy . . .

While the process, with its clear line and frank spaces of colour is attractive to artists, and in harmony with the modern tendency towards colour, yet collectors to some extent fight shy of Colour Prints, dominated as they are by the idea that the reproductive process must be confined to black and white, such as the etching. This prejudice is somewhat strange, because Japanese colour prints fetch high prices and the Japanese are themselves buying them back from Europe.

Mr Morley Fletcher adopted the Japanese method almost exclusively . . . From first to last every step is carried out by hand. No press is used, and indeed printing in watercolour (which gives a mat surface without shine, eminently suited for wall decoration) is only possible by hand rubbing. The colours used are the best artists' watercolours, although the powder form, before being ground with the vehicle such as glycerine and gums, gives the best results. The paper is Japanese, made from the bast or inner bark of the mulberry and unequalled for toughness and durability.

The process is of the simplest, but demanding care and attention to detail. In a way everyone who has dried a blot of ink on the table by placing a piece of blotting paper over it and rubbing the back, has carried out the operation of colour printing in its essentials . . .

Prints are not reproductions of paintings but are themselves originals as etchings are . . . The personal nature of the work might be emphasised. In machine colour printing, once the correct register has been obtained . . . the printing goes on automatically; not so with hand printing. Every time the paper is passed over the block there is the possibility of error, and any carelessness shows itself by faulty registering.

Another distinguished coloured wood-block print artist was NORBERTINE VON BRESSLERN-ROTH who was born in Graz, Austria, in 1891. A precociously gifted child, she studied first at the Art School in Graz and from 1912 to 1916 at the Academy of Fine Arts in Vienna under Professor Schmutzer. At the age of twenty-five, Norbertine Roth married fellow artist George Ritter von Bresslern. Although she was a painter of animals, it was through her multicoloured wood-block prints that she chiefly established her international reputation. At first she made only black prints from her wood engravings. But, inspired by the many coloured Japanese wood-block prints, from about 1919 she began to apply her individual style to this technique. Nature was her constant theme. As Malcolm Salaman says, in his introduction to *The Studio* monograph of her original wood-block colour prints, her theme was 'feather, fur, and fin'. She studied living animals mostly in zoos and rarely went to see them in their natural habitat. Farm and domestic animals and birds also were the subjects of her work.

As Plates 113 and 114 show, her special gift was the ability to simplify the colours, and stylise the postures, of the animals so that they could be rendered in one harmonious print. To convey the sense of the texture and colour of fur or feather by a technique that prohibits exact depiction of detail is particularly difficult. To suggest the characteristic movements of a group of animals or birds in one static image is also difficult. She successfully achieved both.

Although inspired by the Japanese, the coloured wood-block prints in Europe at the beginning of the twentieth century, like those of Seaby and Bresslern-Roth, had a style of their own. They have a clear affinity with contemporary works from the Glasgow School of Art and lack the sophisticated detail of the Japanese works. (For the friendship of Seaby and Crawhall, see page 20.) The technique may have been Japanese but the style was European.

Another European artist making coloured wood-block prints, and with a style completely his own, is painter and sculptor, writer and philosopher, ROBERT HAINARD who was born in Geneva in 1906 and for many years has lived in Bernex, to the west of the city. The old farmhouse where he lives has been surrounded by modern housing but is an oasis of quiet and calm. Along the drive up the hill to the house are large sculptures in various materials, mostly stone, some completed and others unfinished, depicting the wild animals he loves.

He studied under his sculptor-artist father who was a lecturer at the School of Industrial Arts in Geneva. Robert has written and illustrated thirteen books, all except one (concerning his parents Philippe and Eugenie) about nature, the countryside, nature reserves, and science. Two books have been written about him and another two-volume work catalogues his 737 wood-block prints published between 1924 and 1983.

As Robert grew up, he increasingly appreciated the countryside and its wildlife. Throughout his life he has spent very many hours tracking his elusive subjects, chiefly mammals, in the forests of Europe, particularly those near his home. Avoiding the use of a camera, he records what he sees in quick, vivid pencil sketches, including (as every scientist should) the place and date. He has sketched wildlife in Africa and England but he prefers to be near his home.

Having studied under his sculptor father, it was natural for him to begin his career as a sculptor in wood and stone and he has continued to work in these media. However, he has also applied his sculpting skills to the specialised and difficult technique of wood-block colour printing. Hainard makes his blocks by cutting along the grain of the wood rather than across it, so, strictly speaking, his technique is one of using multiple woodcuts to produce his delicately coloured prints. His technique produces an ethereal atmosphere, each picture having diffuse outlines. This effect is partly produced by the paper he chooses and partly by the way he carves his wood and makes his prints.

113   *Bison*
NORBERTINE VON BRESSLERN-ROTH (1891–)
Wood-block print in four colours, 24×27 cm
(9½×10¾ in)

To achieve this charming composition so successfully, the artist has analysed the colours as blocks, some superimposing others. The eyes are particularly successful, ideal in size, colour and exact location

Handdruck.   Bresierus-Rot.

In 1985 I was privileged to see him at his workbench in his sitting-room. His treasured tools were neatly laid out in order on the bench. Accidentally I moved one as I passed the bench. Immediately, he put it back in its proper place. His tools are his long-time, trusted friends and servants. Although he has kept all but one of the sets of printing blocks of each of the very many prints he has ever made, he very generously gave NATURE IN ART the wood blocks from which Plate 115b was produced. There are eight blocks for nine colours, two of which were applied with one block: the red for the beaks and the orange for the feet. He also donated a complete set of the pulls of each individual colour and the preliminary sketch of the scene that inspired the print (Plate 115a).

Next, we consider one more example of relief print making: linocuts. ROBERT GILLMOR was born in Reading, England, in 1936 and has lived there all his life. After five years at the Fine Art Department at Reading University, he taught art and craft at his old school, Leighton Park, from 1959 until he went freelance in 1965. From his youth Robert has been a keen ornithologist and for many years a leading member of the Reading Ornithological Club. He has been Vice-President of the British Trust for Ornithology and the British Ornithologists' Union and a member of the Council of the Royal Society for the Protection of Birds. He was one of the founders of the Society of Wildlife Artists and was elected its President in 1982. He is a Council member of SWAN and active in many other societies and as a lecturer and teacher is much in demand all over Great Britain.

114 *Sulphur-crested Cockatoos*
NORBERTINE VON BRESSLERN-ROTH (1891–)
Wood-block print in four colours, 23×15 cm
(9×6 in)

The acrobatics, colours and form of these birds has been cleverly captured in simplified blocks of colour. With the branches to which they cling, they have been skilfully arranged to make a pleasing composition

115 *Gadwall and Gulls*
ROBERT HAINARD (1906–)
Wood-block print in nine colours, 28.5×37 cm
(11×14½ in), signed and dated Geneva, 11 January
1985

(a) Preliminary pencil sketch
(b) Finished print (overleaf). The quiet colours and
their 'softness' are typical of his work. The raised
wings of the gull on the left are vital to the success
of the composition

151

Robert Hainard

Robert Hainard
Genève, 11 janv, 1985
15/75

Influenced by his famous grandfather Professor Allen W. Seaby (see pages 20, 146), Gillmor has always been interested in graphic design and printmaking. His linocut *Snowy Owls* (Plate 116) makes clever use of only four colours to achieve a simple but strikingly successful design originally created for the cover of *Birds*, the magazine of the Royal Society for the Protection of Birds. Although he is skilled with watercolours, the many demands on his time have prevented him from painting large gallery pictures. He has illustrated numerous books and journals and counts himself very fortunate to be able to earn his living and keep his family by doing work he really enjoys.

116 *Snowy Owls*
ROBERT GILLMOR (1936–)
Linocut in four colours, 38×28 cm (15×11 in)

Charmingly successful, this has excellent composition and colour simplification. How sad that such works are so much more time-consuming to produce than paintings! Very precise registration of each block is essential for such image quality

A/P *Snowy Owls*   *Robert Gillmor*

I cannot leave the pictures at NATURE IN ART without a brief mention of one other painting technique, batik (from the Javanese word for 'painted'), even though it is strictly neither a print nor an oil or watercolour painting. It consists essentially of painting with molten wax on cloth which, between each wax application, is dyed. Quality batik rarely depicts wildlife. At present NATURE IN ART owns only two examples.

BETH ERLUNG, born in Texas in 1947, says she could always draw. After graduation in zoology in 1970, she spent more than two years in Okinawa, Japan. It was there that she first saw and learned the Indonesian method of batik which, she says:

. . . is basically drawing [on cloth] with hot wax to achieve a resist and using dyes . . . to obtain the colors. As I became more adept at drawing with the wax, . . . I wanted to make more realistic pictures . . . My teacher . . . said . . . it could not be done. Being the defiant type of person I am, and probably encouraged by the scientific approach, I set out to the challenge of producing the most realistic batik possible. Ultimately I was able to achieve . . . between thirty and fifty colours.

Take a Breath (Plate 117) was inspired by the underwater scenes Beth often witnessed among the coral reefs of Okinawa:

I loved the experience of the sun shining through the water, causing reflections to play on everything its rays hit, the total quiet with intense visual stimulation. I think whales became a logical choice to depict because I so admire their intelligence, their strength and their gentle nature. Because of the loving relationship between mothers and babies, I believe they serve as an example to humans who need to treasure their young more completely.

I think an artist's role is to stop the action and give new pleasure to the viewer so that he can appreciate what the world is about. As a wildlife artist, I believe it is necessary to promote the conservation of our environment and the plants and animals with which we share that environment.

Many wildlife artists would echo the last two sentences.

117   *Take a Breath*
BETH ERLUND (1947–)
Batik, 41×55.5 cm (16×21½ in)

Something of the still and silent mystery of the oceans and their heaving surface is well conveyed in this scene. The dappled light on both whales and the uneven colours of the sun's rays reaching down into the cold depths add to the drama of the situation. What a privilege to be there!

CONCLUSIONS

One picture is worth a thousand words.

Ancient Chinese proverb

Wildlife art is treasure, well worth discovering and celebrating. Viewing the whole genre in one book, based on one collection, is like trying to capture some magnificent landscape by seeing it through a keyhole. The subject is far too vast and noble to be encapsulated in any one book! But to get even a glimpse of what is beyond the keyhole is better than never to have looked at all. However limited the view has been, this celebration has, I hope, shown that there is an exciting and extensive genre of wildlife art to be explored and enjoyed.

Writing this book has been a pleasure. I am particularly glad to have had the privilege of reading all the personal contributions from the artists who have given something special to it. I very much hope that you, like me, now have a sense of having begun to get to know some of these people as well as having appreciated examples of their work. We have been privileged to see what inspires them and how they approach and do their skilful work. In particular, I am grateful that the artists allowed me to reproduce the exact words which they sent me, even though there has had to be shortening of

some contributions. The sincerity and personality that these statements reveal would have been lost if I had altered them. From the comments of various individuals a consensus of opinion emerges concerning their motivation and inspiration.

Poets seen to have a special sensitivity to the true issues in life and have the precious gift of being able to describe them eloquently. The art of creating a picture with words is akin to that of making one with paint. Peter Partington, who does both, recognised the truth of what Lars Jonnson said: 'a bird . . . in a certain light speaks to me and touches something within me.' Adding his own description of what he saw, Partington says of the inspiration of his watercolour, 'something spoke . . .' Shackleton says, 'if the lovely things . . . are lovely enough, and the artist feels the desire to pay some sort of homage or tribute, something must be astir.' Lennard Sand, referring to his oil paintings, wrote, 'the artist's spiritual awareness colours the painting . . . My urge to paint is conditioned by an insatiable desire to create.' Demonte, painter of flowers, recognised that 'we testify to the spirituality of God present in the natural realm. And we share in a reflection of that spirituality as we create.' Would that more of us were able to recognise as humbly and candidly the reality to which each of these artists is pointing us.

Another motivation is the longing to help people enjoy and protect wild living things. NATURE IN ART certainly endorses the view expressed by Beth Erlund when she wrote, 'I think an artist's role is to stop the action and give new pleasure to the viewer so that he can appreciate what the world is about. As a wildlife artist, I believe it is necessary to promote the conservation of our environment and the plants and animals with which we share that environment.'

By collecting together the work of so many gifted and inspired artists, The International Centre for Wildlife Art, NATURE IN ART, is a starting-point for further exploration of the fascinating 'landscape' visible through the 'keyhole' of this book. The Centre, with its galleries and grounds, makes further study of the subject easy and interesting. There are usually four temporary exhibitions annually, while different parts of the permanent collection are put on display throughout the year and loaned items are also constantly changing, so that there is always something new to be seen. In addition, artists in residence may be seen at work in the studios, and courses are available in the theory and practice of a great diversity of art forms and crafts. Why not send for details? Or, better still, come to see for yourself and celebrate with us!

L'ENVOI

Rudyard Kipling (1865–1936)

When Earth's last picture is painted and the tubes are twisted and dried
When the oldest colours have faded, and the youngest critic has died,
We shall rest, and faith, we shall need it – lie down for an eon or two,
Till the Master of All Good Workmen shall put us to work anew!

And those that were good shall be happy; they shall sit in a golden chair;
They shall splash at a ten-league canvas with brushes of comet's hair;
They shall find real saints to draw from – Magdelene, Peter, and Paul,
They shall work for an age at a sitting and never be tired at all!

And only the Master shall praise us, and only the Master shall blame;
And no one shall work for money, and no one shall work for fame,
But each for the joy of the working, and each, in his separate star,
Shall draw the Thing as he sees it for the God of the Things as They are!

ACKNOWLEDGEMENTS

The production of a book of this kind inevitably involves the kind co-operation of many people, to all of whom I here record my thanks.

I am particularly grateful for the generous help of the many artists mentioned in the text who gave or lent their paintings or prints to the museum NATURE IN ART and allowed them to be reproduced here, gave or lent sketches and other preliminary studies and took the trouble to write, often eloquently, of what inspired their work. Without their personal input this book could not have taken the form it has.

Private individuals have also assisted by allowing me to reproduce works owned by them which they have lent to NATURE IN ART. These include (in numerical order of illustration): Mr & Mrs Richard Mather Plate 4; Greville Mee 18, 19; Mr & Mrs Malcolm Lyle 26; Dr Louise Reid-Henry 47, 55; Mrs Gerth-Pfeiffer 70, 71; Mrs Barbara Saxton 90; and Robert Gillmor 113, 114.

I am similarly indebted to organisations which have lent works to NATURE IN ART and allowed me to include them here: Carlisle Museum and Art Gallery 8; Elsa Wild Animal Trust (founded by Joy Adamson) 20; Rijksmuseum Twenthe, Enschede, The Netherlands 63, 65, 66, 67, 68; and Ruskin Gallery, Sheffield 99.

I am grateful for the kind permission to reproduce pictures owned by or loaned to NATURE IN ART: Shell UK Ltd 16, 17; J. C. Harrison Ltd 26, 27; Tryon and Moorland Gallery 28, 29; the Linnean Society 104; and, for the loan of a transparency, Christie's 15; and Tryon and Moorland Gallery 54. In spite of much effort, I have failed to contact a few artists. To them, or the owners of their reproduction rights, I offer my apologies and thanks.

For translation of oriental texts and advice, I am indebted to Timothy T. Clark and Alec Vans and, for help in finding information and other material, to Sarah Minchin, Curator, NATURE IN ART, and Robert Gillmor.

I am specially grateful for their encouragement to Christine Jackson, who has read and improved the text by many helpful suggestions, and to my ever-patient and enthusiastic wife who has valiantly heard my much talking on this subject for so long.

Last, but not least, I record my thanks to the publishers, and particularly to Faith Glasgow, the editor, who have taken such care in every part of the design and production of this book.

SELECT
BIBLIOGRAPHY

General Texts

Archer, Mildred. *Natural History Drawings in the India Office Library* (Her Majesty's Stationery Office, 1962)

Blunt, Wilfred. *The Art of Botanical Illustration* (Collins, 1950)

Brown, Louise Norton. *Block Printing and Book Illustration in Japan* (Routledge, 1924)

Dance, S. Peter. *The Art of Natural History. Animal Illustrators and Their Work* (Country Life Books, 1978)

Garrett, Albert. *A History of Wood Engraving* (Bloomsbury Books, 1978)

Hammond, Nicholas. *Twentieth Century Wildlife Artists* (Croom Helm, 1986)

Hulton, Paul, & Smith, Lawrence. *Flowers in Art from East and West* (British Museum Publications, 1979)

Jackson, Christine E. *Bird Etchings. The Illustrators and Their Books, 1655–1855* (Cornell University Press, 1985)
Bird Illustrators. Some Artists in Early Lithography (Witherby, 1975)
Wood Engravings of Birds (Witherby, 1978)

King, Ronald. *The Temple of Flora by Robert Thornton* (Weidenfeld & Nicolson, 1981)

Klingender, Francis, (Ed Antal, E., & Harthan, J.) *Animals in Art and Thought to the End of the Middle Ages* (Routledge & Kegan Paul, 1971)

Lane, Richard. *Images from the Floating World* (Oxford University Press, 1978)

Rix, Martyn. *The Art of the Botanist* (Lutterworth, 1981)

Vedlich, Joseph. *The Prints of the Ten Bamboo Studio* (Crescent, ND)

Texts on Specific Artists, Listed Alphabetically by Artist's Name

AUDUBON, J. J. L.
Bell, James B. *John James Audubon. A Selection of Watercolors in the New York Historical Society* (The New York Historical Society, 1985)
Ford, Alice. *Audubon's Animals. The Quadrupeds of North America* (Studio Publications, 1951)

BADMIN, S. R.
Beetles, Chris. *S. R. Badmin and the English Landscape* (Collins, 1985)

BATEMAN, R.
Derry, Ramsay. *The Art of Robert Bateman* (Viking, 1981)
The World of Robert Bateman (Viking, 1985)

BEWICK, T.
Bain, Iain. *The Workshop of Thomas Bewick. A Pictorial Survey* (Thomas Bewick Birthplace Trust, 1989)

BRESSLERN-ROTH, N.
Salaman, Malcolm C. *Masters of the Colour Print. Bresslern Roth* (The Studio, 1930)

CHING, R. See HARRIS-CHING, R.

COMBES, S.
Combes, Simon. *An African Experience. Wildlife Art and Adventure in Kenya* (Clive Holloway Books, 1989)

GOULD, J.
Sauer, Gordon C. *John Gould. The Bird Man.* (Lansdowne, 1982)
Lambourne, Maureen. *John Gould. Bird Man.* (Osberton, 1987)

HAINARD, R.
Anker, Valentina. *Robert Hainard. Les Éstampes.* Tome 1 1924–56, Tome 2 1957–83. (Xylon-Verlag, 1983) [737 prints listed]

HARRIS-CHING, R.
Hansard, Peter. *Wild Portraits* (Airlife, 1988)

KEULEMANS, J. G.
Keulemans, T., & Coldewey, J. *Feathers to Brush. The Victorian Bird Artist John Gerrard Keulemans 1842–1912* (Limited edition of 500 published by the authors, 1982)

KUNHERT, W.
Van der Loeff, M. J. *De Schilderkunst van Wilhelm Kunhert* (Van der Loeff, Enschede, 1957)

LEAR, E.
Noakes, Vivien. *Edward Lear. 1812–1888* (Weidenfeld & Nicolson 1985)

LILJEFORS, B.
Hill, Martha. *Bruno Liljefors. The Peerless Eye.* (Allen, Kingston upon Hull, 1987)

MEE, M.
Morrison, Tony (Ed) *Margaret Mee. In Search of Flowers of the Amazon Forests* (Nonesuch Expeditions, 1988)

PERKINS, B.
Perkins, Benjamin. *Trees* (Century, 1984)

REDOUTÉ, P-J.
Mallary, Peter & Frances. *A Redouté Treasury. 468 Watercolours from Les Liliacées of Pièrre-Joseph Redouté* (Dent, 1986)

REID-HENRY, D
Henry, Bruce. *Highlight the Wild* (Palaquin, 1986)

SCOTT, P.
Scott, Peter. *Observations of Wildlife* (Phaidon, 1980)
Benington, Jonathan (Ed) *Sir Peter Scott at 80. A Retrospective* (Alan Sutton, 1989)

SHACKLETON, K.
Shackleton, Keith. *Wildlife and Wilderness. An Artist's World* (Clive Holloway, 1986)

SHEPHERD, D.
Shepherd, David. *David Shepherd: The Man and his Paintings* (David and Charles, 1985)

THORBURN, A.
Southern, John. *Thorburn's Landscape. The Major Natural History Paintings* (Elm Tree Books, 1981)

TUNNICLIFFE, C. F.
Gillmor, Robert. *Charles F. Tunnicliffe, RA. The Composition Drawings Catalogue.* (Bunny Bird Fine Art and Tryon & Moorland Gallery, 1986)
Niall, Ian. *Portrait of a Country Artist. Charles F. Tunnicliffe, RA, 1901–1979* (Gollancz, 1980)

WILSON, A.
Cantwell, Robert. *Alexander Wilson, Naturalist and Pioneer* (Lippincott, 1961)

WOLF, J.
Palmer, A. H. *The life of Joseph Wolf Animal Painter* (Longmans, 1895)

INDEX